Part I
All About Bettas

The Betta

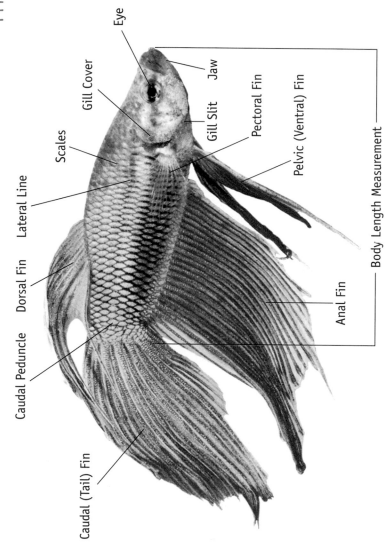

Eye

Jaw

Gill Cover

Scales

Gill Slit

Pectoral Fin

Lateral Line

Pelvic (Ventral) Fin

Dorsal Fin

Body Length Measurement

Caudal Peduncle

Anal Fin

Caudal (Tail) Fin

Chapter 1

The Jewel of the Orient

Imagine for a moment a cheerful and brightly colored aquarium. The wispy, delicate leaves of a green aquatic plant sway gently in the filter's current. The translucent floating leaves of a dwarf water lily dapple the light streaming in from above. As your eyes drift toward the center of the tank, you notice a bright red Betta with majestic, flowing fins moving casually along as it patiently surveys its surroundings. Darting in and out among the plants, a school of Harlequin Rasboras patrols the depths below. Sounds inviting doesn't it?

This is the enchanting realm of the Betta, one of the most beautiful inhabitants of the tropical aquarium. If the fascinating world of tropical fish delights and amazes you, then you and I share a passion that has captured the hearts of a wide variety of hobbyists for over a century. Withstanding the test of time, the Betta quickly became a favorite choice among freshwater aquarium keepers, and has remained popular for many years. Keeping a Betta will give you and your family years of never-ending enjoyment, and it provides the perfect introduction to tropical fishkeeping. Creating an underwater world that is diverse in color and form rewards tropical fishkeepers with years of pleasure.

Satisfaction, relaxation, and pride go hand in hand with success in the aquarium hobby. You will experience that success when you learn how set up and maintain a healthy aquarium for your new Betta. Come along as we explore the amazing world of the Betta together.

These Pearl Gouramis belong to the same family as the Betta.

The Betta Family

Bettas belong to the family of labyrinth fish *(Anabantidae)*. A structure known as the labyrinth organ enables them to breathe atmospheric air, a valuable trait in waters that are low on dissolved oxygen. Other members of this unique family include Gouramis *(Trichogaster, Colisa)*, Paradise Fishes *(Macropodus)* and the Climbing Perch *(Anabas testudineus)*, which can even use its air-breathing ability to move short distances across land.

In their homeland waters of Thailand, Bettas live in shallow rice paddies, stagnant pools, polluted streams, and other places where the water has a low oxygen content. In these locales, the water temperature can reach 90 degrees Fahrenheit under the direct rays of tropical sunlight. Thus, in nature Bettas live in warm, stagnant water.

In the aquarium Bettas prefer water that is 79 to 82 degrees Fahrenheit—slightly warmer than the water temperature favored by other freshwater tropical fish, which prefer a temperature between 76 and 78 degrees Fahrenheit. Bettas also prefer quiet currents, unlike fish that are naturally found in flowing streams and rivers. Successful aquarium keeping always involves providing conditions in the aquarium similar to those the fishes encounter in nature.

A History of Betta Keeping

Undoubtedly, fishkeeping began when fish were first maintained in ponds or containers as part of the food supply. But no one knows exactly when people first started keeping fish in containers purely for enjoyment. The bright colors of some fish may have led people to regard them as special, perhaps in the same way that colorful gems came to be valued more than drab-colored rocks.

Thai workers refer to the Betta as "the jewel of the Orient." Wild Bettas have plain colors compared to their gaudy modern descendants, but perhaps a rare colorful fish turned up in fishing nets from time to time. Considered, perhaps, a token of good luck, the fish would be kept in a bowl and cared for. We don't know for sure how keeping Bettas started.

> **T I P**
>
> Almost anyone can keep tropical fish—even people who live in apartments or in small homes where other types of pets, such as cats and dogs, are not practical or are prohibited.

We do know the history of the scientific study of this fish. The Betta (*Betta picta*) was first described in 1846 by French biologists Valenciennes and Cuvier. After the first shipment arrived in the United States in 1909, C. Regan gave this marvelous fish the scientific name *Betta splendens*.

The beautiful Betta varieties found in today's tropical fish market are the descendents of Asian stock, selected by breeders for vivid colors and long, elegant fins for more than a century. Americans such as Warren Young have also contributed much to the production and development of the long-finned and highly colorful Bettas that you can buy today. Young developed the Libby Betta, the prototype of the large variety of strains that are now available. These brilliant new strains no longer resemble the plain-looking wild Bettas from which they were originally developed.

Commercial breeding offers the hobbyist plenty of choices among a wide range of patterns and fin styles. Most tropical fish dealers stock Betta varieties to match almost any individual taste.

Betta Fighting

Thai people call the Betta *pla kat,* which means "tearing or biting fish." No doubt rice paddy workers saw nest-guarding males defending their territories against all comers, most notably other male Bettas seeking territories of their

Fighting Fish

Wild Bettas selectively crossed with more aggressive-natured domesticated species yield champion fighters. Placed together in a suspended glass bowl where neither can escape, they do what comes naturally to a male Betta when confronted with a competitor. They fight. Large monetary bets are placed on these competitions—explaining, in part, why such cruel spectacles endure.

Organizers seldom permit the two Bettas to fight until one kills the other. Nevertheless, many die shortly afterward from injuries sustained during the bout. Fortunately, Betta fighting is illegal in the United States.

own. Their pugnacious tendencies led to their use in the sport of Betta fighting. Even today in the United States, the colloquial name for the Betta is Siamese Fighting Fish.

The wild Betta differs in many respects from the captive-bred fighting fish. The fighting fish is stockier and has a pug nose. The wild Betta rarely fights—usually only to defend territories or mating partners. Such ritual fights, limited to threatening displays of flared gills and spread fins, are mostly for show and confrontations rarely end in death. One male gives up and retreats. Better to find another, even a less desirable place to raise a family than to die and raise no offspring at all.

In the home aquarium, a Betta's aggressive behavior toward other males of the same species will be intensified because of confinement and the lack of escape routes. Only one male Betta should be kept in an aquarium. Female Bettas rarely fight with each other. Once in a while a little fin nipping and other acts of bad temper take place among squabbling females, but usually little or no serious damage ensues. In general, it is not advisable to place a male and a female Betta together in a community aquarium, because it is possible that other innocent tankmates may be injured if the pair decide to bicker or spawn.

None of this should discourage keeping a Betta with other types of community fish. Tankmates for the Betta should be non-aggressive. Rasboras, Danios, small Barbs, and a host of other popular aquarium fish originating in Asian

These two males are squaring off. Only one male Betta should be kept in an aquarium.

habitats often make the best companions. Beware of Cichlids and large Barbs that can become fin nippers. A fish that decides to take a small taste of a Betta's beautiful fins may chase it to the point of exhaustion and collapse.

A Suitable Environment

Because of the Betta's reputation for physical hardiness, many hobbyists make the mistake of providing Bettas with inadequate living accommodations (small glass bowls and jars) and poor water conditions. While it is true that a Betta may be capable of living for several years (actually just surviving) in a small bowl of cool water, it will reach full coloration and robust health only in a properly designed aquarium.

Bettas deserve the same good care and quality aquarium conditions as all other species of tropical fish. In an aquarium with warm water and a good filtration system, your Betta can achieve its full physical potential and be happy. And making your Betta healthy and happy is what this book is all about.

You can easily see the effects that good living conditions have on your fish's health. Set up a small aquarium according to the guidelines in this book. Then

Arrangements like this may look beautiful, but they are not healthy for your fish. Bettas deserve the same good care and quality aquarium conditions as all other species of tropical fish.

purchase one of the Bettas lurking lethargically in small bowls at your local fish dealer. Take the Betta home and place it in your well-maintained aquarium. Within a matter of hours, you will notice an increase in coloration, activity level, and alertness as your Betta happily settles into its new home.

Chapter 2

Betta Basics

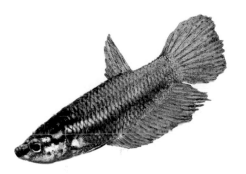

As is the case with other species of fish, body form largely determines the Betta's lifestyle. A fish's shape, mouth structure, and fin design can tell us a lot about the way it lives, eats, and moves through the water. When you gain a basic understanding of how fish evolve to maximize their chance of survival in their natural habitat, you will be able to look at an unfamiliar species and make an informed guess about its aquarium requirements.

What Is a Betta?

Ichthyologists (people who study fish) classify fish based on body form and structure. They group species in a hierarchy of ever more inclusive categories, from individual species such as *Betta splendens* to families (such as anabantids, which are fish with a labyrinth organ), to a large class, Pisces, that includes all fish. Fish represent but one class of vertebrates (animals with backbones, including humans). Other vertebrate traits include a brain case (skull) and a skeleton that protects the internal organs and supports the body weight.

Like all fish, the Betta breathes through external gills. Like other anabantids, it also has the labyrinth organ that enables it to use atmospheric air.

Body Shape

A Betta's streamlined body enables it to slip smoothly and effortlessly through the water. The tapered shape reduces friction, conserving the Betta's energy as it quickly moves to catch its prey. Fish that have a more rounded shape, such as fancy Goldfish, swim more slowly and tire easily. Such fish often live in running water, where the current can aid their movements.

The turned-down mouth of a Catfish means it is destined to pick food from the bottom of rivers, ponds, and aquariums.

Fish that live in stagnant or slow-moving waters in their natural habitat develop a flattened, compressed body shape to facilitate gliding through stands of the upright reeds and plants that also favor such environments. The Discus *(Symphysodon)*, which lives in quiet shallows along the Amazon River, provides a similar example. In fast-running water, a fish shaped like the Discus would get tossed about in the current like a leaf.

Mouth Structure

The shape of a fish's mouth may largely determine its mode of life. For example, you'll find a turned-down mouth (inferior position) on bottom-dwelling species such as Catfish. These fish feed in mud, sand, or gravel, and off flat rock surfaces and plant leaves. A mouth located in the terminal position points directly forward from the fish's face. Common among species such as Guppies and Platys that swim in midwater levels, a terminal mouth facilitates "picking off" food as it sinks toward the bottom or floats in the water column.

The Betta's upturned mouth, known as the superior mouth position, enables it to feed efficiently at the surface. Bettas snatch small insects and mosquito larvae from among the floating vegetation in the pond or paddy. They also greedily scoop up flakes at the top of the aquarium.

Always take care to ensure that your Betta receives its fair share of nourishment, especially if it is living in a tank with faster swimming, more aggressive fishes. Add food that sinks together with food that remains on the surface. Don't force your Betta to compete with mid- and bottom-dwelling tankmates at feeding time.

The Betta's Lifestyle

Bettas prefer warm temperatures and gentle currents. They feel most secure when the aquarium provides plants that root in the bottom as well as plants that float on the surface. Betta tank-mates should be non-aggressive fish that won't harass the Betta or nip its fins. Bettas feed on a variety of small insects, mosquito larvae, and worms that they pluck from the surface of the water. In the aquarium they thrive on flakes, freeze-dried and frozen brine shrimp, live mosquito larvae, or other foods that tend to stay near the top of the water column.

Scales

Scales cover the Betta's body, overlapping each other like the shingles on the roof of a house. These thin, transparent scales help protect the Betta's body from injury and streamline the fish for efficient swimming. A mucus layer covers the scales, reducing drag as the fish swims (this is the slimy feeling you get when you hold a fish in your hands). The mucus also helps protect against invading parasites and infection.

The Betta's scales lack pigment. Its brilliant colors actually come from pigment cells located in the skin. The skin also produces both the scales and the mucus covering.

Swim Bladder

The Betta's body weighs slightly more than the volume of water it displaces, so it tends to sink. So, like many other fish, the Betta has a gas-filled swim bladder that functions as a flotation device.

By making minor adjustments to the gas pressure inside the swim bladder, the Betta can remain suspended (neutrally buoyant) with little or no effort. If the Betta moves to the bottom of the tank, its swim bladder will be compressed and it will begin to sink. To correct this problem, the Betta must either add gas to its swim bladder to achieve neutral buoyancy again, or use energy to swim upward.

The opposite is true when the Betta moves toward the top of the tank. There, it must release gas from the swim bladder or must use energy to return to a deeper depth. Gas enters or leaves the swim bladder via a specialized duct. As the

The fancy Betta varieties, such as this splendens, *have long, flowing caudal fins.*

Betta moves about in its watery realm, small changes inside its body, unseen by the human eye, automatically maintain the proper buoyancy.

Fins

Bettas use their fins not only to move through the water, but also to steer and to maintain their balance. The fins are composed of long rays with skin stretched thinly between them. Special muscles attached to the rays provide control. Your Betta's fins include one caudal fin, one dorsal fin, two pelvic fins, one anal fin, and two pectoral fins.

The caudal or tail fin, combined with the muscular tail stalk, provides the force for sudden forward bursts of speed and for fast swimming. In fancy Bettas, such as the *splendens* varieties, the lengthening of the natural caudal fin through artificial selection (breeding for a specific trait) has resulted in a slower-moving species than its native relative.

The sole purpose of the dorsal fin (located on the upper back region) and the anal fin (on the bottom) is to give the Betta stability, in the same way the tail assembly on an airplane keeps it stable. These fins keep your Betta in an upright position and prevent it from literally rolling over in the water.

Pectoral fins also provide stability while moving through the water and help the fish steer. Located near the bottom of the fish, directly beneath the gill openings, the pectoral fins can also be used by the male Betta to fan its incubating eggs, bathing them with fresh water to eliminate wastes and debris.

Pelvic fins are located on the hip area and also aid in stabilization and steering.

Color

The Betta's color is produced by pigment cells (chromatophores) in the skin. In the wild, coloration may help camouflage a fish from predators or may advertise its presence to potential mates. Wild Bettas do not possess the vibrant colors (bright red, lime green, royal blue) of their captive-bred counterparts. Fanciers have selectively bred Bettas to achieve fish with a wide range of colors and long, flowing fins. The males will develop much brighter colors than the females, and they exploit their bright coloration in mating displays designed to attract and impress females.

The Betta's chromatophores occur in successive layers within the skin. To produce a Betta of a specific color, the other colors layered on top must first be stripped away through selective breeding to expose the desired color beneath. The top color is blue; next is red, then black, and finally yellow.

Wild Bettas lack the vibrant colors of their captive-bred counterparts.

Their tail fin provides most of the propulsion for these female Bettas.

Body Functions

Respiration

A fish's gills extract life-giving oxygen from the water. Water is pumped through the mouth and then across the gills, flowing over the gill filaments, which are richly supplied with capillaries. Blood flowing through the capillaries absorbs oxygen and releases harmful carbon dioxide. Depleted of its oxygen and laden with wastes, the water then passes to the outside through the gill cover, or operculum.

The typical fish can remove up to 85 percent of the oxygen from the water taken in through the gills. Active fish, such as Danios, must continuously swim forward to force water across their gills to obtain enough oxygen for survival. These types of fish survive in a constant state of near asphyxiation if they are placed in a small aquarium that restricts their free-swimming movement. Swimming languidly, on the other hand, the Betta needs less oxygen than a Danio does, and so tolerates more confinement.

A Betta's main respiratory device is its labyrinth organ, located just behind the gills. See page 24 for more about this special organ.

Movement

Water surrounding its body provides a fish with ample support. Therefore, little energy is needed to overcome the force of gravity in water as compared to that needed by animals on dry land.

As in many other fish, the tail fin provides most of the Betta's propulsion by pushing water around it backward, which, in turn, propels the Betta forward.

Orientation

Bettas orient themselves by sight alone, interpreting the direction from which light comes as "up." If you shine a flashlight into the side of an otherwise darkened tank, the Betta will usually swim sideways, positioning itself appropriately to the false "up" position. Change the direction of the light again and the Betta will orient accordingly.

Osmosis

Fish maintain the proper levels of dissolved salts within their body cells by controlling the amount of water they absorb. Freshwater fishes, such as the Betta, maintain a higher level of salt than that of the water in which they live. Thus, they constantly absorb water, endangering the delicate balance of their body chemistry.

The fish's kidneys remove water in the form of dilute urine, which is excreted. A fish suffering from kidney failure often swells grotesquely due to excessive water absorption. Still, some salt is required to maintain normal body functions. Special salt-absorbing cells located in the gills move salt from the water into the blood, maintaining the appropriate balance. Small amounts of salt contained in food also help the Betta to keep its salt content in balance.

Marine fish (fish that live in salt water) have the opposite problem. These species must constantly ingest water to replace that which is lost to the saltier environment around them. If they do not "drink" enough they will die, ironically, from dehydration.

A Betta's Senses

Vision

Each one of the Betta's two eyes, located on opposite sides of the head, produces a different image. This is known as monocular vision. A Betta (which can focus on objects up to about a foot away) finds it difficult to focus both eyes on a single object. It therefore lacks depth perception.

In humans, the shape and curve of the eye lens is constantly changing in order to achieve proper focus. In a Betta's eye, the lens remains the same shape. Ligaments focus the image by moving the lenses backward or forward, like a bellows on an old-fashioned camera.

Do Bettas Sleep?

A Betta lacks eyelids, so it can't close its eyes for a good night's sleep. Instead, when your Betta tires, it will rest either by lying with its abdomen on the gravel or by hanging motionless in the water, just floating. The swim bladder automatically maintains this position. Bettas sleep for short periods at various times during the day and night, so perhaps we should say they take frequent naps.

A Betta cannot adjust to rapid changes in brightness, because the iris works too slowly. Thus, it will act "shocked" and panic when an aquarium light is turned on or off suddenly. To avoid this, always turn the room lights on or off before turning the aquarium light on or off.

Lateral Line

Because it has relatively poor vision, the Betta relies on its lateral line to locate nearby objects. The lateral line runs down the Betta's side from the back of its eye to the base of its tail fin. Small holes along the lateral line enable water pressure to affect specialized nerve endings. The pattern of water pressure, which is influenced by the shape, size, and movement of objects in the vicinity, stimulates the nerves to signal the brain. The fish's brain interprets the nerve signals as an image of the Betta's surroundings, enabling it to find food, avoid obstacles, and detect the stealthy movement of a predator.

Hearing

Each of the Betta's ears is composed only of a simple inner chamber, because sound in water travels much faster than it does in air. Vibrations that are picked up from the Betta's environment pass over the sensory components in the chamber to provide sound. Scientists believe the swim bladder also works together with the Betta's inner ear to amplify and distinguish individual sound patterns.

Taste and Smell

A Betta's taste buds are located on the mouth, lips, and fins. Smells are taken in through the nostrils. Both senses serve the Betta's needs by responding to chemicals in the water. Such chemicals can signal the presence of food or warn of an approaching predator. The Betta can only detect chemical sensations over a short distance. Therefore, it must constantly forage to find enough food—unlike some fish, such as sharks, that can sense the taste of a potential meal from miles away.

The Labyrinth Organ

In the wild, Bettas live in poorly oxygenated water, such as swamps and rice paddies. The Betta's special labyrinth organ evolved to extract oxygen from the air when needed. The labyrinth is a unique respiratory organ and is found in the suborder *Anabantoidei*, which also includes the Paradise Fish and the Croaking Gourami.

The labyrinth organ enables oxygen to be absorbed from the air directly into the bloodstream. Many fish can swallow air and absorb oxygen through the gut lining. An outgrowth of the gut, the labyrinth organ appears to be an evolutionary refinement of this technique and clearly provides a survival advantage in the often oxygen-poor habitats favored by anabantid fishes.

The labyrinth is located inside the head, just behind the gill section. This organ consists of rosette-shaped plates containing thousands of blood vessels

Paradise Fish also have a labyrinth organ to extract oxygen from the air.

that absorb oxygen from air the fish has inhaled. The winding shape of this organ is the basis of the name labyrinth, which means "maze." The multiple folds of the organ maximize the surface area available for oxygen absorption.

Because Bettas breathe air, they can survive in less space than the average tropical fish can. (Water holds much less oxygen than the same volume of air.) This enables commercial breeders to keep the males in separate compartments until they are ready to be shipped.

Unfortunately, many hobbyists believe that because of this unique physical characteristic, Bettas can be kept safely in crowded conditions. Fishkeepers must remember that Bettas add the same amount of waste to the water that other fishes do, and are just as susceptible to disease brought on by overcrowding and poor water conditions.

Bettas should never be kept in small bowls for long periods of time. It will benefit their health in the long run to keep them in larger aquariums that offer plenty of swimming space and stable water conditions.

Chapter 3

Bettas and Their Tankmates

Although most aquarium fish are now bred in captivity for sale, in their natural habitats they are found throughout the world. The diversity of these fish is amazing. To make them easier to understand and sort out, scientists have classified them into various groups.

A particular species has a common name, which can differ depending on the region or the language. However, every species also has a scientific name that is used to identify that species in all places and all languages. The scientific name of a species is based on Latin, and is made up of the genus name and the species name. For example, the scientific name of the Neon Tetra is *Paracheirodon innesi* and the Cardinal Tetra is *Paracheirodon axelrodi.* The first name is the genus (a grouping of very similar species), and in this case both Tetras belong to the same genus, *Paracheirodon.* In fact, if you look at these fish, you can see that they are extremely similar. The second name refers only to that species and no other. Similar genera (the plural of genus) are classified into families.

Varieties of Bettas

Most dealers offer the common Betta, *Betta splendens,* as a regular fish in their inventory. The other Betta species listed here may be more difficult to locate. Dealers can sometimes order the others. Also check online for possible sources.

Sarawak Betta *(Betta akarensis)*

The Sarawak Betta has a small, rounded tail and short fins. The female is usually a flat bronze color. The male can be distinguished by the dark stripe down the length of its side.

Pearly Betta *(Betta anabatoides)*

The Pearly Betta has a spade-shaped tail and short fins. The female is a dull bronze color with dark splotches and the male is a brighter bronze with a touch of green on the fins. The male also has a dark stripe that runs straight from the eyes to the gills.

Slender Betta *(Betta bellica)*

The Slender Betta has a spade-shaped tail and short fins. It is predominantly pink. The female has dark dots on the tail and fins. The male has a touch of green over the body and fins. Other colors include orange with a smattering of green, and a green-blue with a touch of pink. All have dotted tails and dotted dorsal fins.

His dark stripe tells you this Sarawak Betta is male.

Edith's Betta (Betta edithae)

Edith's Betta has a rounded tail and short fins. The female is dull orange with dark splotches and white spots. The male is a brighter orange with dark splotches. Spots on the male are blue-green and appear in the same pattern as the female's.

Foershi's Betta (Betta foershi)

Foershi's Betta has a rounded tail and short fins. The female is pink-orange with dark splotches running from front to back. The male is also orange. The male's splotches are green, and his gills are bright orange.

Peaceful Betta (Betta imbellis)

Among the less frequently seen species, this one is perhaps the most commonly available. It has a rounded tail. The fin sizes vary, but the pectoral fins are always long. The body of this Betta is predominantly dark with blue-green markings. Its most distinguishing characteristic is that the edge of its tail fin is a bright red. The pectoral fins are red with blue-green tips. The end of the anal fin is red as well. The dorsal fin is almost always a blue-green color. One other significant marking is the appearance of blue-green stripes on the tail.

Brunei Betta (Betta macrostoma)

The Brunei Betta has green edging around the dorsal and anal fins. This species has a rounded tail and small fins. Body color can range from gold to pink and white. The white Brunei has two dark stripes that run from its head to its tail. The pectoral fins are always green. The pink Brunei will have a red stripe on its tail (see photo on next page).

Painted Betta (Betta picta)

The Painted Betta has a rounded tail and small fins. This Betta is usually gold and has three dark stripes that run from head to tail. All the fins are edged in green.

The Five Most Popular Betta Species

1. Fighting Fish (Betta splendens)
2. Peaceful Betta (Betta imbellis)
3. Emerald Betta (Betta smaragdina)
4. Mouthbrooding Betta (Betta pugnax)
5. Slender Betta (Betta bellica)

This pink Brunei has the characteristic red stripe on its tail.

Mouthbrooding Betta *(Betta pugnax)*

The Mouthbrooding Betta has a round tail and very small fins. A few have pointed tails. Colors on this fish vary considerably, ranging from a light gray to an orange-gold. Because its colors are so varied, the Mouthbrooding Betta often looks as if it swam through a rainbow.

Emerald Betta *(Betta smaragdina)*

The beautiful emerald Betta has a rounded tail and very large fins. The body color in this species is usually a deep vibrant green overlaid with a black web design. The long pectoral fins are tipped in red. The caudal fin is red with green or blue lines.

Siamese Fighting Fish *(Betta splendens)*

The Siamese Fighting Fish is the most common Betta seen in pet stores. The caudal fin comes in a variety of shapes (rounded, pointed, spade, split, double, lace, comb) and is usually long and flowing. The oversized anal fin can range from being cut close to the body to extending almost 3 inches out. The color range of this fish is similar to the selections at a paint store. (The large variety of individual color patterns will be discussed later in this chapter.)

The Mouthbrooding Betta comes in many colors, from light grey to bright orange.

The bright green Emerald Betta is aptly named.

Splendens, *the classic Siamese Fighting Fish, is the most popular Betta species.*

The dark stripes and pink and orange colors distinguish this Tessy's Betta.

Betta splendens is the species most often exhibited at fish shows. It is not unusual for breeders and hobbyists to travel great distances in their search for a Betta of a certain color—often for very obscure reasons. I personally know one woman who traveled more than 500 miles just to find a *splendens* that would match the color of the drapes in her living room.

Banded Betta (Betta taeniata)

The Banded Betta has a round tail and small fins. Colors in this species run from a dull gold to tarnished copper. The body is banded, with flecks of green.

Tessy's Betta (Betta tussyae)

Tessy's Betta is a unique blend of pink and orange. It also has three dark stripes in a zigzag pattern. The fins on this species have flecks of green throughout.

Betta Color Patterns

There are six major color patterns found in Bettas, and these help hobbyists identify particular variations of a species. As time passes and new strains of Bettas are bred, they will be given new pattern names if they do not fit into the existing categories. The following descriptions should give you an idea of what to look for when you are searching for a particular pattern. Note that many hobbyists and breeders disagree on exact pattern definitions.

- A **solid-colored Betta** will have one color (bright red, royal blue, orange, or gold) that basically covers the entire body and fin areas. Solid coloration may be marred by imperfections (small specks of white or other colors), which breeders are working to eliminate.
- A **bicolored Betta** has a body that is one solid color with fins that are a lighter or darker variation of the same color. For example, a Betta with a light blue body and dark blue fins would be considered bicolored.
- A **Cambodian Betta** has a body of one color and fins of another. For example, the body on this type may be red, while all the fins are light blue.
- A **butterfly Betta** has a body of one color that blends into the fins near the torso area. The outer edges of the fins are a different color.
- The **Cambodian-butterfly Betta,** as its name suggests, is a cross between a Cambodian and a butterfly Betta. The body on this Betta

Bettas can be kept happily with most peaceful species of fish.

will be of one color, while the fins will have two different colors. For example, the Cambodian-butterfly can have a red body with blue and gold fins.

- A **marbled Betta** is unique. The body and the fin tips are the same color. The inner portion of the fins is a different color, which gives this Betta a striped appearance.

Tankmates for Bettas

For a truly splendid Betta tank, I prefer a design that mimics the Betta's habitat, complete with fish and plants that might be found together in the wild.

Despite the fact that male Bettas fight viciously among themselves, a single male Betta rarely bothers other fishes in the community aquarium. Bettas can be successfully kept with most peaceful species of fish. Common choices include the many kinds of Tetras, small Catfishes, and livebearing fishes such as Guppies, Platies, and Swordtails. The species listed below all come from Southeast Asia.

Coolie Loach *(Pangio kuhlii)*

Grubbing about in the soft bottom mud beneath quiet water after dusk, the Coolie Loach usually rests among vegetation during the day. The dark brown body is attractively marked in yellow-orange bars from the snout to the base of the tail fin. This species makes a good scavenger for the Betta tank, as it will seek out food missed by the other fishes. In the wild, it grows to about 6 inches, but aquarium specimens are usually about half that size.

Glass Catfish *(Kryptopterus bicirrhus)*

The fascinating Glass Catfish is almost completely transparent. The internal organs can be clearly seen through the body wall. It does best in groups. Individuals usually remain together, hovering tail down among plants in midwater. A docile species, the Glass Catfish should not be kept with active, aggressive tankmates. These fish will often orient themselves facing the outflow from a power filter. In the wild, this behavior positions them to snatch food carried by the current.

Rasboras *(Rasbora spp.)*

The genus *Rasbora* includes some of the best aquarium fishes found in Southeast Asian waters. All remain small, seldom reaching 2 inches long. Schooling fishes that swim among dense plant growth, they eat most types of aquarium foods

Glass Catfish do best in small groups.

Livebearers and Egglayers

In general, most experts prefer to combine freshwater aquarium fish families into two major groups: livebearers and egglayers. This is based purely on the method these fish use to reproduce. The livebearers give birth to live young. They include four major families—*Anablepidae*, *Goodeidae*, *Hemirhamphidae*, and *Poeciliidae*—that are kept in captivity. These are the common aquarium fish known as Guppies, Mollies, Platys, and Swordtails, as well as the various breeds and strains of each. These are especially hardy fish that breed readily in captivity. The males of these families are easily recognizable by their gonopodium. This modified pelvic fin is used by the male to mate with the female.

Most species of fish, including Bettas, lay eggs. Different egglayers have different reproduction strategies, some of which involve watching the eggs and even caring for the young. Rasboras, Catfish, and Loaches are all egglayers.

with relish. Temperature and pH requirements are the same as for Bettas, making them good choices for tankmates.

- The **Harlequin Rasbora** *(R. heteromorpha)* turns up in almost every dealer's inventory from time to time. Pinkish-orange body coloration is accented by a black triangle at the base of the tail and the red-orange dorsal fin.
- Another relatively common species, the **Scissortail Rasbora** *(R. trilineata)* has a torpedo-shaped body. Its silvery scales have dark edges. A dark stripe runs from the midpoint of the body to the base of the tail. The outer tips of the tail fin have a yellow-black-yellow pattern of three spots. When the fish moves its tail, the moving spots give the illusion of a pair of scissors opening and closing.
- It's worth looking for the **Red-Tailed Rasbora** *(R. borapetensis)*. Like others in the genus, its peaceful habits and ease of feeding make it an ideal tankmate for the Betta. The silvery body has a pair of stripes running from the eye to the base of the tail. The upper stripe is golden yellow, the lower one is black. The base of the tail is blood red.

- **Clown Rasboras** *(R. kalochroma)* seldom school, unlike other Rasboras. In the aquarium they are peaceful and lively, darting in and out among the plants. The slender, brick red body has a black spot just behind the gill cover and another, larger black spot below the dorsal fin.
- Seldom exceeding an inch in length, the **Pygmy Rasbora** *(R. maculatus)* is also a perfect tankmate. Peaceful, it schools among plants in ponds and ditches. The red-orange body is marked with three black spots: one behind the gill cover, another near the anus, and the third at the base of the tail fin.

Blue Gourami (Trichogaster trichopterisi)

Close relatives of the Betta, Gouramis require the same aquarium care. Also known as the Three Spot Gourami, this peaceful fish grows to about 4 inches long and makes a great companion to the Betta in a sufficiently large aquarium. Males can be distinguished from females by the shape of the dorsal fin: His is pointed and elongated toward the tail; hers is much shorter and rounded at the tip. Several color variations of the Blue Gourami are available. This is an extremely hardy species that takes all common aquarium foods.

Croaking Gourami (*Trichopsis* species)

Members of the genus *Trichopsis* do not turn up that often in aquarium shops. They are lovely little fish, seldom exceeding a few inches in length. One, the Dwarf Croaking Gourami, *T. pumila*, tops out at 1 inch. With lovely red and blue coloration and long, pointed fins, it is worth adding a pair to your community tank if you can find them. The dorsal fin of the female is rounded and shorter than that of the male.

Dwarf Gourami *(Colisa lalia)*

The Dwarf Gourami male rivals the Betta for bright coloration, and its red and neon blue markings become even more intense at breeding time. In this and other Gourami species, the pelvic fins are elongated and threadlike. The fish use them to explore the surrounding environment. Dwarf Gouramis reach only about 2 inches in length.

Pearl Gourami *(Trichogaster leeri)*

Pearly white dots on a dark background make this fish appear to have been colored by an Impressionist painter. The throat and belly of the male are tinted red, and his coloration intensifies during courtship. Found in heavily vegetated rivers, this fish grows to 4 inches. If you have a 30-gallon tank or larger, you could include a pair in your Betta aquarium.

Part II
Setting Up the Aquarium

Chapter 4

Understanding Aquarium Equipment

You'll need to consider many factors, including cost, what the other people in your household think, and your available space, before you buy an aquarium setup. You may want to put your aquarium in an area of your home where everyone can enjoy it, or perhaps putting it in a quiet spot or a room that's just yours would be best. In particular, the amount of money, space, and time you have to devote to the aquarium will greatly affect your final decision.

Things to Think About

More than anything else, the size of the tank you buy will determine not only the initial cost, but also the time you will need to maintain it, the space needed to accommodate it, and the long-term expense of your aquarium.

Financial Considerations

Larger tanks require larger equipment, which will cost more than the same equipment for a smaller aquarium. Take the time to make a few quick trips to your local fish dealer; these information-gathering excursions will give you a general idea of how much each particular setup will cost.

After the aquarium is completely set up and running, bear in mind that you will also need to buy additional items such as food, nets, test kits, maintenance equipment, and so on. With these thoughts in mind, the best advice is always to buy the largest aquarium you can afford. You will be able to keep more fish, and the larger initial outlay repays you handsomely with fewer maintenance problems, healthier fish and plants, and more years of enjoyment.

Space Considerations

An important factor to consider when choosing your aquarium is the amount of space you will have at home for the tank. If you live in a small apartment, for example, a 10- or 20-gallon tank may be all you can accommodate. If you live in a large home, you may have a little more area to work with and you might be able to buy a bigger tank, such as a 40- or 55-gallon one, without cramping your living space.

The table below will give you a general idea of the overall dimensions of several standard size aquarium tanks. Remember, this is only the size of the tank itself—the stand and the other equipment will also take up space.

Tank Sizes

Tank Capacity	Tank Shape	Dimensions (L × W × H, in inches)
10 gallons	Regular	20 × 10 × 12
	Long	24 × 8 × 12
15 gallons	Regular	24 × 12 × 12
	Long	20 × 10 × 18
	Show	24 × 8 × 16
20 gallons	High	24 × 12 × 16
	Long	30 × 12 × 12
25 gallons	Regular	24 × 12 × 20
30 gallons	Regular	36 × 12 × 16
	Breeding	36 × 18 × 12
40 gallons	Long	48 × 13 × 16
	Breeding	36 × 18 × 16
45 gallons	Regular	36 × 12 × 24
50 gallons	Regular	36 × 18 × 18
55 gallons	Regular	48 × 13 × 20
65 gallons	Regular	36 × 18 × 24
75 gallons	Regular	48 × 18 × 20

Where to Put an Aquarium

Place the aquarium in an area of your home that is free from cold drafts and direct sunlight to keep the water from overheating or chilling. Basements and garages (unless they are well-insulated and heated) are therefore poor choices, as is the kitchen and any location near windows or doors. Avoid any space that is drafty or where the temperature changes rapidly or unexpectedly.

Do You Need a Divider?

For years, plastic or glass dividers have been used to partition tanks so two or more male Bettas can live in the same aquarium without being able to interact aggressively. A divider can also be used to separate males and females in a breeding tank. Using a divider totally destroys the natural look of an aquarium, though, so do remember that you only need one if you keep more than one male Betta or want to try breeding. Make sure the divider you buy has small holes in it so that water can flow through easily.

If you want to keep several male Bettas at a time, you might consider buying a few smaller tanks instead of getting just one large aquarium that would require dividers. However, a larger tank is more suitable to use as a community aquarium with a single Betta and several peaceful tankmates.

These females can live together peacefully, but two males in the same tank will fight.

Tank Types

Aquarium hobbyists have lots of choices when it comes to tanks, support furniture, and equipment. Today's retail market can accommodate almost anyone's décor, space, and budget.

Glass Tanks

All-glass aquariums are still the most popular. Made of plate glass and sealed with nontoxic silicone that allows for expansion when the tank is filled with water, glass tanks resist scratching and provide a good viewing area. One disadvantage of glass is the difficulty of drilling holes for filter parts—something that is easily accomplished with acrylic tanks.

Glass tanks are also much heavier than acrylic tanks and can be difficult to move, especially when the tank is large. The glass must be increasingly thicker as the tank size gets larger to support the increased water pressure. Glass tanks can break, too, leaving you with a huge mess to clean up. Fortunately, such disasters are rare.

> ### CAUTION
>
> **Building Your Own Tank**
>
> Avoid the temptation to build your own tank, unless you really know how to make a secure and safe aquarium. Working with glass can be dangerous, and it is much better to buy a tank than to flirt with water leaks and other such disasters that often accompany aquariums built by inexperienced hobbyists.

Acrylic Tanks

Acrylic tanks come in a seemingly infinite number of amazing shapes and sizes. Far lighter than comparable glass tanks, acrylic aquariums can be drilled with ordinary woodworking tools, if necessary, to install equipment.

Acrylic aquariums cost more than all-glass tanks and scratch more easily. Scratch remover products on the market will cover most simple blemishes caused by cleaning and carelessness.

An acrylic tank creates a small amount of visual distortion, due to the bending of the material during construction. These bends, however, give the tank an appealing, seamless look.

Tank Shapes

Glass tanks are almost always rectangles of some sort. Acrylic aquariums, however, can be molded into a number of fascinating shapes, including rectangles,

The more top surface area a tank has, the more room for gas exchange. A tall, narrow tank or a bowl, such as the one above, has a smaller surface area than a shallow, wide tank.

squares, hexagons, octagons, tubes, fish-eyes, bubbles, and L-shapes. When choosing the shape of your tank, keep several concerns in mind.

The oxygen content of water is related to the surface area of the tank and the temperature of the water. Warmer water has less oxygen than colder water. Since Bettas prefer warmer water, the amount of oxygen in the tank may be limited. But vital oxygen must enter the tank, and toxic carbon dioxide must leave it, or the fish will suffer.

Gas exchange occurs at the water surface—the top of the tank. The more surface area a tank has, the more room for gas exchange at the surface—more opportunity for oxygen to enter the water and toxic gases to leave. Therefore, the larger the surface area of the tank, the more fish the tank can hold.

An aquarium's shape affects the surface area. A tall, narrow tank has a small surface area and will accommodate much less gas exchange than a shallow, wide tank, which has a larger surface area.

The surface area of the aquarium also determines the number of fish that it can hold. Each fish needs oxygen to survive, and each produces waste carbon dioxide. A healthy aquarium demands enough surface area for proper gas exchange.

In the wild, Bettas live in shallow pools that are wider than they are deep. Accordingly, a standard rectangular aquarium will not only provide good surface area for gas exchange, but will also allow sufficient swimming space.

Tank Size

To ensure that your new fish have an adequate surface area for stable water conditions, I suggest a 20-gallon tank as a good starting size. With that said, the larger the tank, the better, unless you plan to keep only one Betta and a few companions. Water conditions tend to remain more stable as tank size increases.

> ## Buying Secondhand
>
> If you decide to buy a secondhand tank, be sure to inspect your purchase carefully for leaks, cracks, and silicone breakdown. When buying used tanks from a retailer, check to see if the silicone seal is complete and uninterrupted. Even a small break in this seal can eventually cause leakage. An aquarium with old sealer can, however, be salvaged. Simply remove the old silicone with a razor blade (please exercise great care when using a sharp instrument!) and then replace it with new sealer. Leave the new sealer to dry for at least forty-eight hours before you add any water to the tank.

The larger volume of water resists major temperature fluctuations. Wastes accumulate more slowly. Your Betta (and all fish) benefits from such conditions.

Tank Weight

The weight of the tank is an important factor in deciding what tank to buy. Fresh water weighs about 8 pounds per gallon. Thus, a 20-gallon tank would weigh roughly 160 pounds—without equipment! Make sure you get a sturdy stand for your new tank and distribute the weight of the tank as evenly as possible over strong flooring.

Determining Aquarium Capacity and Weight

Here's an easy way to figure out about how much a fully loaded aquarium (including fish, gravel, equipment, and the like) will weigh. Start by finding the tank's capacity. To do that, simply measure the length, width, and height of the tank and use the following formula :

$$\text{Capacity (in gallons)} = \text{Length} \times \text{Width} \times \text{Height (in inches)} \div 231$$

For example, suppose you have a tank that measures 24 inches long by 12 inches wide by 16 inches high. Twenty-four times 12 times 16 equals 4,608; divided by 231, you end up with about 20 gallons of water. This is the capacity.

Now, multiply that 20 by 8 to find the weight of the water—160 pounds. (Remember, fresh water weighs about 8 pounds per gallon.) Allow another 20 percent for the weight of the tank itself and the equipment. That's another 32 pounds, bringing the total to 192 pounds. Don't forget to add in the weight of the substrate you'll be placing in the tank. Figure 2 pounds of substrate per gallon of water, or 40 pounds in this example. That brings the total aquarium weight for a 20-gallon tank to 232 pounds. Acrylic tank setups will weigh a little less, but this is a good way to make a general estimate.

Substrate

The substrate or gravel in your tank plays an important role in the biological cycle. Beneficial bacteria grow along the top of the gravel bed and will help break down waste in the aquarium. Gravel is also useful for anchoring live plants and holding down decorations.

When selecting substrate, neutral-colored, natural gravel products are the best choice. Brightly colored gravel competes with the natural beauty of your Betta. In addition, your fish will feel much more comfortable in a natural-looking environment. A more natural environment helps reduce stress and will promote spawning and other natural behaviors.

Plants like this Java fern do best in a substrate with smaller grains.

Substrate Size

Avoid large-grained substrate materials. Food can get trapped between the pebbles, fouling the water and creating a maintenance headache.

Plants tend to do best in a medium- to small-grained substrate. Gravel with individual particles about ³⁄₁₆ of an inch in diameter, mixed with about one-third coarse sand, offers

TIP

Basing the gravel calculation on the bottom area of the tank makes more sense than figuring so many pounds of substrate per gallon of water, as is sometimes recommended. A little more or less, by the way, won't do any harm.

the best compromise between the needs of the plant roots and ease of maintenance. You can strew a few larger pebbles on top for decorative effect, if you like.

How Much Substrate?

Live plants need about 2 inches of substrate. If you plan on using plastic plants, limit the substrate to an inch. A 5-pound bag of gravel will cover about 40 square inches at a depth of 1 inch. For the 20-gallon tank in our earlier example, we have 288 square inches of bottom to cover ($24 \times 12 = 288$). Since a 5-pound bag covers 40 square inches, you need to divide 288 by 40 to see how many 5-pound bags you need. The answer is about seven, or a total of 35 pounds of gravel for 1 inch of substrate. You'll need to buy double that (70 pounds) for 2 inches of substrate.

Filtration Systems

Filters play an essential role in the biological cycle of your Betta's aquarium. At its most basic, an aquarium filter system promotes biological filtration and removes debris from the water. Some filters can perform mechanical, chemical, and biological filtration all at the same time. (The box on page 48 explains these three types of filtration.) Because most models release water bubbles, they also aerate the water.

Corner Box Filter
Biological, Chemical, Mechanical Filtration

One of the oldest devices in the aquarium hobby, the corner box filter was originally designed for small aquariums. This filter contains a single airstone (see chapter 5) attached to a pump that pushes water through layers of activated charcoal and floss contained in a plastic box. The filter itself rests on the gravel bed inside the tank.

Three Types of Filtration

Biological Filtration

In an aquarium, bacteria convert deadly ammonia from fish waste and food debris to nitrites and nitrates. This critical conversion process is known as the nitrogen cycle, and it will be described more fully in chapter 5, "Ready for Setup." The nitrogen cycle is the essence of biological filtration. Every surface in an aquarium that is in contact with the water develops a film of nitrifying bacteria. Filters are often designed to provide additional surfaces for colonization by bacteria to maximize the effect of biological filtration.

Chemical Filtration

Chemical filtration is the removal of dissolved compounds from the water. For example, aquarium filters often include a compartment that holds activated carbon to absorb dissolved minerals as water passes through the filter. Various other filter media can also be used to remove undesirable compounds.

Mechanical Filtration

Mechanical filtration is the removal of particulate debris. Debris produces cloudiness and an untidy appearance. Materials such as polyester fiber floss, plastic foam, or sponges capture debris as water is pumped through them. Over time, the surface areas of all these media become covered with beneficial bacteria, and they then function as biological filters, as well.

Corner filters are inefficient because they take a long time to filter all the water in the tank. They can also be noisy and may float around the tank if they are not weighted down properly. A more efficient power filter is a better choice.

Power Filter
Biological, Chemical, Mechanical Filtration

Power filters come in a wide variety of sizes and usually have one or two slots that hold fiber pads containing a small amount of activated carbon. They offer

Proper filtration will keep your tank clean and healthy, enabling your Betta to fully develop its rainbow of colors.

major advantages. The equipment and replacement pads are inexpensive. Changing the pads is quick and simple on most models.

The simplest power filters hang on the back of the tank. Water enters through a siphon that extends nearly to the bottom of the aquarium. An electric pump pulls water through the filter pads and returns it to the tank via a spillway.

Choose a model that accepts two filter pads and change only one at a time. This way, you do not throw away all your beneficial nitrifying bacteria each time you toss out a pad.

Canister Filter

Biological, Chemical, Mechanical Filtration

Like the simple power filter, a canister filter contains several media compartments through which the aquarium water is drawn by a pump. Water usually enters and leaves the tank via hoses connected to the filter. Hiding the hoses among plants and decorations is easy, enabling you to create a more natural scene in your aquarium. Rapid water turnover and a larger volume of filter media result in greater efficiency than can be had with a hang-on-the-back filter. For a large tank, a canister filter may be your wisest investment.

TIP

Safety First

When cleaning your tank or rearranging the décor, *always* unplug all electrical equipment first.

Undergravel Filter
Biological, Mechanical Filtration

The undergravel filter was once the standard for biological filtration. This type of filter consists of perforated plastic plates that sit on risers about an inch above the bottom of the aquarium. Two to six plastic uplift tubes fit into holes in the base plates. In the simplest design, an airstone at the bottom of each uplift is supplied from an electric air pump. As bubbles rise in the uplift, water is pushed along. This causes aquarium water to flow downward through the plastic plates. Newer models use a small water pump, known as a powerhead, to suck water up through the lift tubes, providing better turnover. Powerheads can be adjusted to regulate the speed of water currents produced. The outlet often swivels to direct the water flow as desired.

With this arrangement, the substrate itself is the filter medium. Oxygenated water flowing through the gravel brings ammonia to the beneficial bacteria living on every grain. Mechanical filtration results when debris becomes trapped in the gravel bed.

A reverse-flow undergravel filter draws water through a mechanical filter, then passes it back down the uplift tubes to be distributed throughout the aquarium after it is pushed up through the gravel bed. A reverse-flow system increases the efficiency of the undergravel filter and the longevity of the bacterial colony, primarily because it reduces debris accumulation that restricts the water flow.

The major drawback to both undergravel designs is that debris accumulates in the gravel bed. Eventually, regular vacuuming (using a special aquarium vacuum tube) of the gravel becomes necessary to maintain an optimal flow, regardless of the direction the water moves.

Fluidized Bed Filter
Biological Filtration

Compact fluidized bed filters use sand as the filter medium. Water pumped through the filter keeps the sand suspended as a loose slurry. The sand provides an enormous amount of surface area on which beneficial bacteria can multiply. Constantly tumbled in the flowing water, the sand becomes what is known as a fluidized bed. The sand grains are always surrounded by oxygenated water, resulting in an excellent transfer of ammonia to the bacterial film. Gas exchange is also facilitated by this design.

A fluidized bed filter will respond quickly to extreme changes in ammonia levels caused by overstocking and overfeeding, but for routine aquarium filtration it may be more trouble to maintain than other types of filters.

Sponge Filter
Biological Filtration

A sponge filter draws aquarium water through a large sponge that acts as a biological medium after beneficial bacteria gather on its surface. This type of simple filter is often used in quarantine, hospital, and fry tanks.

Heaters

There are two types of aquarium heaters: submersible and non-submersible. Submersible heaters are entirely encased in a watertight glass tube. Non-submersible heaters hang on the tank's frame; the glass tube rests in the water, but the unit must never be fully submerged. Both types work the same way: A thermostat turns the heating element on and off in response to the temperature, just like your furnace. Always follow the manufacturer's directions to set the temperature to the desired range. (For Bettas, the range is 79 to 82 degrees Fahrenheit.)

The right light will keep both your plants and your fish healthy.

TIP

Avoid Incandescent Lighting

Tungsten (incandescent) lighting is generally found in the standard light bulbs that are used in the lamps around your home. It is *not* suitable for the aquarium. It has a short lamp life, produces too much heat, has uneven output, and has a limited spectrum.

A general rule for determining heater size is to get 5 watts of heater per gallon of water. So a 20-gallon aquarium needs a heater that is at least 100 watts.

Always make sure to unplug the heater when you remove any water from the tank. If the heater turns on while it is dry, it may get hot enough to crack when you put it back in the water.

Thermometers

Your Bettas need a fairly consistent water temperature, and the only way to be sure they are getting it is with a thermometer. Stick-on aquarium thermometers consist of a peel-and-stick plastic rectangle applied to the outside glass near a corner. Liquid crystal film between the layers of plastic lights up in different spots as the water temperature changes.

Glass or plastic aquarium thermometers filled with red alcohol come with suction cups or hangers to secure them inside the tank. You read the temperature as you do with an ordinary fever or weather thermometer. Place the thermometer where you can easily see it but where it won't detract from the scene inside the tank.

Lighting

Light plays an important role in your Betta's internal biological clock, helping to determine both feeding and spawning patterns. Your Betta will need a cycle of day (lighting) and night (darkness) to imitate the conditions of its native habitat. You can connect the aquarium lights to a timer to keep the cycle regular even when you are not around.

Fluorescent Bulbs

Fluorescent lighting is the best choice for the Betta aquarium. It fosters plant growth, has a long lamp life, and does not produce a lot of heat. If you are growing live plants, install two fluorescent tubes that are the same length (or as close as possible) as the tank. If you have no plants, a single tube will do.

Extra Aquarium Equipment

These extra items might come in handy for your aquarium.

Scissors
Plastic household scouring pads
Scrub brush
Plastic buckets
Assorted sponges
Extra towels

It's best to have separate cleaning buckets, sponges, and brushes that you use only for your aquarium. This way, there will be no residue of toxic household cleaners that might harm your fish.

Plan on replacing fluorescent tubes once a year, whether or not they have burned out, because they grow dimmer with time.

Metal Halide Lights

Metal halide lights provide plenty of intensity for vigorous plant growth and produce a pleasing visual effect in the aquarium. On the downside, they produce a lot of heat and are expensive compared to a fluorescent system. For a large tank with sun-loving plant varieties, though, metal halide lighting should be your first choice.

Covers and Light Hoods

Aquarium dealers supply two types of lighting arrangements. The simplest includes a glass cover that fits into a lip molded into the plastic trim at the top of the tank. Across this, a long, narrow plastic fixture, called a strip light, holds one or two fluorescent bulbs.

The more elaborate arrangement, called a hood, completely covers the top of the tank. Lighting equipment is mounted inside the hood. Metal halide units and larger fluorescent units should have a ventilation fan to prevent overheating. Dealers offer hoods designed to match the aquarium. Choosing such an ensemble lends a finished, professional look to the tank, making it blend in well with home décor.

Other Equipment

In addition to the basic equipment, there are a number of smaller items you will need to buy. (For a complete list of everything you will need to start your aquarium, see the Shopping List at the beginning of this book.)

Nets

Nets are available in a variety of sizes and designs. Smaller nets are generally used for catching fry and little fish. The fine webbing in these nets is soft and similar in structure to cheesecloth. Small nets are also handy for scooping out uneaten food and suspended debris from the water.

Larger nets are usually used for capturing fish. You will find that using two large nets to capture a Betta is much easier than trying to do the job with only one. Your fish can easily be coaxed into the center of one net by gently nudging it with the other. You should buy several nets of different sizes so that you will be prepared to handle almost any task.

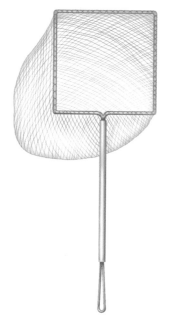

A net is handy for a variety of tasks. You'll probably need several nets in different sizes.

Scrapers

A scraper is a great tool that can be used to remove algae from the aquarium glass. Most scrapers come with a two-sided head. One side has a soft sponge for wiping away loose algae. The other side of the scraper contains a tough scrub pad for removing encrusted algae and lime deposits. Most scrapers are made of plastic and have a long handle for reaching difficult spots in the aquarium. The other end of this tool looks like a small fork and is great for turning over gravel and planting.

Siphons

Siphoning unwanted debris from the tank is a regular part of good maintenance. The siphon can be simply a length of plastic hose. Place one end in the water and the other in a bucket on the floor. Suck on the lower end to start water flowing. Hobbyists squeamish about this procedure will find self-starting and even electrically powered siphons in their local aquarium shop.

A handy accessory for cleaning the gravel bed consists of a long funnel, wider in diameter than the hose, attached to the intake end of the siphon. This design enables water and fine debris to be siphoned out, while leaving heavier gravel or sand on the bottom. I find this gadget to be a good investment.

Change some water and siphon out debris once a week and your tank will remain sparkling clean and healthy. Some hobbyists like to do a larger water change and more thorough vacuuming every month, as well. Choose a routine that suits your schedule and stick with it. (For more on maintaining a healthy tank, see chapter 9, "Healthy Tank, Healthy Fish.")

Test Kits

To keep tabs on your water conditions, you will need to have a few test kits handy. You will need a nitrite test to monitor the progress of conditioning the tank (as described in chapter 5). For routine testing, kits for pH, nitrate, and water hardness complete your aquarium laboratory.

Chapter 5

Ready for Setup

Now that you have all your equipment, it's time to put your aquarium together. Sitting at home, surrounded by all the boxes of equipment and their instruction booklets, setting up an aquarium may seem like rocket science. But it's not. Take a deep breath, then proceed step by step. Be sure to read all the manufacturers' instructions carefully as you go.

The Stand and Tank

The first step is to place the stand in its permanent position. The best support for the heavy weight of the aquarium and all its components is a commercially manufactured aquarium stand. This type of support is built to hold a full aquarium. Commercial aquarium stands will safely handle the weight and shape of the tanks for which they are designed. Don't experiment. Follow the manufacturer's recommendations for installation.

Homemade stands and other furniture may look sturdy, but can fail under the heavy load. Stand failure can be costly to the aquarist and the homeowner (and the fish), so don't try to save money on your aquarium stand. Avoid using furniture as an aquarium stand. The construction may not be up to the challenge, and unforeseen water leaks can quickly ruin the finish.

The aquarium stand should be placed on a sturdy floor. If you live in an apartment, mobile home, or old house, always check the floor and its supports. If in doubt, have a contractor inspect the floor.

Stands that include a built-in cabinet are great for storing unsightly equipment. Retailers stock cabinets in a variety of finishes and designs to complement most any décor. If the aquarium is located in your family living space, you may want to consider buying a cabinet.

Electrical Considerations

Keep in mind that your aquarium will require several electrical outlets. I have known hobbyists who have set up their complete aquarium system and then added water, only to find out that there was no electrical plug anywhere near the tank!

An outlet strip with four to five outlets works great for an aquarium system. Select one that provides a ground fault circuit interrupter (GFCI). This device monitors the current and shuts off the power in the event of an accident, and it can save your life. Building codes often require GFCI outlets for wet areas, such as bathrooms. Consider having an electrician replace the outlet or breaker serving your aquarium if you can't find a plug-in GFCI strip.

> **TIP**
>
> **Moving Your Tank**
>
> *Never* attempt to move a full aquarium, no matter how small it is. A slight shift in weight and water pressure may break the glass. Drain the tank first.

A word of caution: Never attempt to wire aquarium equipment or wall sockets yourself. Contact a professional.

Prefill Cleaning

Once you have the stand in place, it is time to clean your aquarium tank. Never use any type of cleaning product that is not made specifically for aquariums. A little bit of warm water and a sponge will normally do the job. If the tank has lime buildup on the glass, moisten it with a little vinegar and remove with a scraper. Rinse well. After your tank has been thoroughly cleaned, it is ready to be placed on the stand.

Supporting and Placing Your Tank

When you set up your new tank, place a thin layer of Styrofoam beneath the bottom for support. The Styrofoam will compensate for any irregularities in the aquarium's bottom surface. Do not forget to leave space between the tank and the wall for any equipment, such as power filters, to which you will require access for maintenance.

It's a big job to move an aquarium and it always involves draining the tank. So think hard about where you want to place the tank before you start adding everything to it.

Adding Substrate

Wash all the gravel before adding it to your tank. Place batches of gravel in a bucket and run water over it while you mix it up with your hands or a large spoon. Continue to rinse the gravel until the rinse water runs clear.

Slope the substrate so it is higher in the back of the tank than it is in the front. The substrate in the back of the tank should be about half an inch higher than the front. That way, waste material and uneaten food will tend to gather toward the front of the tank, where it can be easily removed.

Decorations

A bare aquarium is not pleasant for your fish or for you. You'll find information about aquarium plants in chapter 6, "Plants for the Betta Tank." There are also other ways to decorate your aquarium and provide interesting places for your fish to hide and forage.

Rocks

Aquarium supply stores sell a variety of tank decorations that enhance the habitat for your fish. Some are plastic or ceramic creations and others are simply attractive rocks and stones. By buying these tank decorations from the dealer, you are avoiding contaminating your tank with toxic substances and water chemistry-modifying agents. Avoid the temptation to collect your own rocks

until you know how to identify each
kind and its influence on your
aquarium.

If you add rocks to your aquarium, place them so they won't topple. Never lean rocks up against the
side of the tank for support, because
they can fall and injure your Betta or
break the glass. Smooth, waterworn
stones look natural in the aquarium; angular blocks do not. In addition, smooth
stones don't have sharp, rough edges that could hurt your fish.

One way to create a permanent and safe effect is to glue rocks together using
a silicone aquarium sealer. This will keep your rock display in place if burrowing
bottom dwellers begin to dig around them. Always allow the sealer to dry for
several days before you place the assembly in the aquarium.

> **TIP**
>
> Always lift an aquarium by placing
> your hands underneath the bottom
> corners of the tank. A larger aquar-
> ium will require at least two people
> to move it.

Wood

Large pieces of driftwood make great centerpieces for an aquarium. It is best to
buy pretreated wood from an aquarium shop. Collecting driftwood yourself

Smooth rocks and large pieces of driftwood make great aquarium decorations.

poses risks, because improperly treated wood can decompose and foul the tank. Over the years, I have found that collecting and treating my own driftwood is not worth the trouble and risk.

Backgrounds

Light streaming in through the back of the tank disorients your Betta and makes it difficult for you to see into the tank clearly. Installing a background helps to eliminate movement and shadow that can frighten your Betta and will provide it with a little extra security. A dark blue or black background can give the impression of endless water depths beyond the aquarium scene. Aquarium shops sell backgrounds that are photographs of underwater plants, driftwood and so forth. These can be extremely effective, visually, if you buy plants and other decorations that continue the background's theme.

Aeration

While a sufficiently large aquarium with a good filter usually provides enough aeration for a Betta, some hobbyists err on the side of caution by installing an airstone connected to a small air pump. The stream of bubbles rising through the tank adds a decorative touch, too.

In the wild, Bettas live in stagnant water. While they will adapt to a gentle current, aeration in the aquarium should not be so overpowering that your Betta is forced to expend all its energy fighting strong currents. Position decorations to provide an obstacle to the direct flow from the pump. Lush plantings also help to slow water movement and achieve the natural calm your Betta prefers, without sacrificing filtration efficiency.

Air Pumps

Inexpensive air pumps can be found in any aquarium shop. Your air pump should sit above the aquarium, if possible, to avoid any backflow of water if the power is shut off. You may want to get a valve to control the air flow. Placing a single valve in line with the pump restricts the flow, but it also makes the pump work harder. It may become noisy and will require more frequent replacement. Instead, use a dual valve. Connect one to the airstone in the tank and use the other to bleed off excess air pressure into the atmosphere.

Wild Bettas live in stagnant water, so if you do decide to add aeration, keep the currents gentle.

Airstones

Airstones increase oxygenation in the water by dispersing the air supplied by the pump. Aquarium dealers sell airstones made of wood, plastic, and ceramics. Depending upon the material, airstones require replacement every few months.

Tubing

Aquarium tubing made of silicone/rubber material is easy to work with. Tinted blue-green by the manufacturer, it blends in nicely, virtually disappearing under water. Rubber tubing can be bent around decorations without kinking and does not crack with age. To slide tubing easily onto the pump outlet or the stem of an airstone, hold it briefly under very hot tap water to soften it slightly. It returns to normal when it cools.

Water Quality

Once you have placed the substrate and a few decorations into the tank, it is time to add water. To make sure water conditions remain optimal for your Betta, you will have to test and condition the water.

Temperature

As I pointed out in chapter 1, the Betta aquarium should be maintained at 79 to 82 degrees Fahrenheit. Cooler temperatures may result in loss of appetite, lethargy, disease, and starvation. Proper filtration and circulation prevent cold pockets from forming in the water.

When the water is within the correct temperature range, your Betta will act alert, eat ravenously, and display brilliant color. A cold Betta will lurk in corners, clamp its fins, and remain inactive.

Chlorine

City water departments add chlorine and chloramine to drinking water to elim-inate harmful bacteria and to make it safe for human consumption. However, these chemicals can be deadly to your aquarium fish and must be removed. Bottled chlorine remover, which you can buy at your local aquarium shop, will neutralize the chlorine and chloramine in your tap water. Simply follow the label's directions and add the chemical to the water before any fish or live plants are put into the aquarium.

Another way to remove chlorine is to aerate the water for 12 hours or let it sit in open buckets for 48 hours. However, bottled chlorine remover works in seconds.

pH Values

Check the pH (a measure of alkalinity or acidity) of the water when you first set up your tank, and afterward every week or two. In a freshwater system such as your Betta tank, pH values can fluctuate rapidly. Even small changes in pH can stress your Betta and make it more susceptible to various types of diseases.

The pH scale ranges from 0 to 14. Zero is the highest acidic level. Fourteen is the highest level of alkalinity. A neutral pH of 7 is neither acidic nor alkaline.

Your Betta will prefer water with a pH between 6.5 (slightly acidic) and 7 (neutral). Most other fish that would make good Betta tankmates can live com-fortably within this range.

The pH in your aquarium can be measured with simple test kits that are available at almost any aquarium store. Most kits consist of a color card, a plas-tic measuring tube, and chemicals. These kits are quite simple to use.

Correcting the pH with chemical additives can become a never-ending chore. Most aquariums, when properly maintained, become slightly acidic, a condition suitable for the vast majority of common tropical fish species. Besides, if you buy fish in your hometown, chances are they are swimming in the local tap water at the store. If the fish show signs of normal health and activity, you needn't fuss too much about pH.

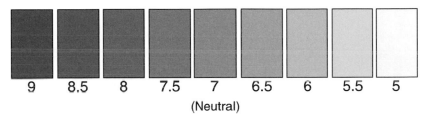

| 9 | 8.5 | 8 | 7.5 | 7 | 6.5 | 6 | 5.5 | 5 |

(Neutral)

Test the pH of your aquarium with a kit available at the aquarium supply store. Your Betta will prefer water with a pH between 6.5 and 7.

Water Hardness

The dH (degree of hardness) is simply the amount of dissolved mineral salts in the aquarium water. You can check the hardness of your tap water with a simple aquarium test kit. Bettas prefer soft water with a dH of less than 25. One way to dilute hardness is to add distilled water from the grocery store. Reverse osmosis units will also reduce hardness, but they are expensive and use a lot of tap water to produce a small amount of mineral-free water. Consider using one only if you need to soften a lot of water.

The Nitrogen Cycle

With any new aquarium, it is vitally important to condition the water that goes into the tank to provide your new pets with the best possible chance of survival. This is a natural biological process, and it takes time.

Fish excrete ammonia, which starts accumulating in the water as soon as you add the fish to the tank. Biological filtration converts this deadly ammonia into less dangerous nitrites and then, later, into even safer nitrates. Beneficial bacteria carry out these chemical conversions, and the conditioning process largely consists of establishing a population of beneficial bacteria in the aquarium.

During the conditioning process, several types of bacteria multiply rapidly over a period of months, literally feeding on the toxic chemicals in the water. As the number of bacteria increases, they can convert larger amounts of waste products into relatively harmless nitrate.

Eventually, though, the nitrates will build up to the point where they can begin to affect your fish's health. The best way to remove nitrates is to change the water frequently (more about that in chapter 9, "Healthy Tank, Healthy Fish").

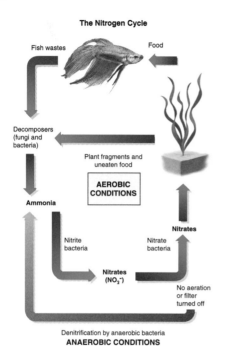

The Nitrogen Cycle

Fish wastes

Food

Decomposers
(fungi and
bacteria)

Plant fragments and
uneaten food

**AEROBIC
CONDITIONS**

Ammonia

Nitrates

Nitrite
bacteria

Nitrate
bacteria

Nitrates
(NO₂⁻)

No aeration
or filter
turned off

Denitrification by anaerobic bacteria
ANAEROBIC CONDITIONS

Conditioning Time

Conditioning time varies depending on the temperature of the water and the type and number of filtration units used. This period may take anywhere from three weeks to several months. The process will begin only after your starter fish have been introduced into the tank. A few hardy species, such as Guppies or a single Betta, should be added to the new aquarium to start the conditioning of the biological filter.

Ammonia levels begin to peak within seven to fourteen days, and eventually the helpful bacteria increase in numbers to detoxify the ammonia into nitrites. Next, the nitrites will accumulate to higher levels and other types of bacteria will begin to convert them to nitrates. Eventually, nitrite levels drop and the conditioning period ends. Nitrate levels will continue to slowly increase over time, but can be maintained at proper levels through frequent water changes.

Monitoring Water Conditions

During the conditioning period, monitor the nitrite level daily. Initially, no nitrite will be present. As the ammonia-converting bacteria begin to multiply, the nitrite level will rise as ammonia is converted. Within a couple of weeks to a month, the nitrite level will peak and then begin to decline. This event signals the development of nitrite-converting bacteria, which grow more slowly than the ammonia-converters. As nitrite becomes nitrate, you will observe a precipitous decline in nitrite. When the level of nitrite reaches zero, the conditioning process is complete.

A check of the nitrate level at this point will reveal that the level, originally zero, has now risen considerably.

Adding Fish

After the conditioning process is complete, you can begin adding a few fish every few weeks to allow the bacteria to increase at a normal rate. If you make the mistake of immediately overstocking your aquarium, you will begin to notice a gradual buildup in ammonia levels again. That's because the ammonia-converting bacteria have not had time to adjust to their new food supply. This can stress both the established inhabitants and the new fish. Avoid the temptation to stock too many fish too soon.

With a little patience, you can condition your new aquarium without any unnecessary loss of life. After that, a few simple weekly tests and regular partial water changes will suffice to maintain a healthy aquarium.

Chapter 6

Plants for the Betta Tank

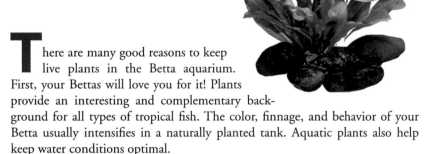

There are many good reasons to keep live plants in the Betta aquarium. First, your Bettas will love you for it! Plants provide an interesting and complementary background for all types of tropical fish. The color, finnage, and behavior of your Betta usually intensifies in a naturally planted tank. Aquatic plants also help keep water conditions optimal.

Plants shelter shy Bettas from more aggressive tankmates. They provide shade, helping to reduce algae growth. Plants also help to condition the tank water by removing carbon dioxide, sulfur substances, and nitrogenous wastes. The biological filter converts ammonia into less-harmful nitrate, which the plants, in turn, use for food.

Purchasing Plants

Most aquarium supply stores stock a wide variety of live aquarium plants. Aquatic plants are supplied as cuttings, as rooted clumps, and in small plastic pots.

Buy plants from a reputable dealer, just as you would your Betta (see chapter 7, "Bringing Your Betta Home," for more on choosing a dealer). Plants in the dealer's tank should look healthy, with sturdy, bright green leaves and no yellowed or rotting portions. Look closely for small snails crawling around in the plant tank. They eat algae and debris, but can multiply to plague proportions and start munching your carefully tended aquatic garden, too. Before you buy anything, have a good idea of the particular types, sizes, and number of plants you will need to achieve the effect you want in your aquarium.

How Many Plants?

If they are provided with good growing conditions, aquatic plants spread and multiply quickly. As a general rule, allow one plant for every 6 square inches of bottom area. If your tank is 12 inches wide and 24 inches long, as in the example in chapter 4, you have 288 square inches of bottom area.

$$288 \text{ square inches} \div 6 = 48$$

That's a total of 48 plants. Use common sense when making the final calculations, though, because some plants are naturally fuller than others and will take up more space. It's better to start with just a dozen plants and add more as your aquarium garden matures.

Plants should be kept constantly damp during the journey home. The best way is to have them bagged in water, as you would a fish. When you arrive home, carefully lay out the plants in a pan of warm water so you can examine them more closely.

Yes, plastic plants look pretty real. But they can't help condition the tank water by removing carbon dioxide, sulfur substances, and nitrogenous wastes from the water. Only real plants can do that.

Aquascaping

It is much easier to place plants into the aquarium after most of the water has been added than to try to arrange them in a dry tank. A partially full tank will enable you to get a better view of the final arrangement after the plants have spread out.

The substrate in a planted tank should consist of fine gravel or coarse sand, so water can circulate around the plants' roots. Plants should be spaced far enough apart that they have room to grow without crowding and shading each other.

If you buy cuttings that are too long for your tank, trim the bottom stem to the length you want. Strip the leaves off the bottom to leave 2 inches of bare stem, and bury the stem in the gravel. Roots will develop in a few weeks.

Rooted plants should be buried just up to the point where the leaves emerge from the root mass. Make sure you do not push the plants too far into the gravel, because deeper planting may cause them to rot. The crown (the area where the leaves emerge from the roots) should be just above, or at, gravel level.

Floating plants merely sit on the water surface and pose few problems. Plants that require attachment, such as the Java fern, can be carefully tied to a piece of driftwood using nylon fishing line. The fern will attach itself after a few months, and the fishing line can be removed.

To begin aquascaping, start by putting the tallest plants near the back of your tank. Next, fill in the center areas with short, bushy plants. Taller bushy plants can be used to hide tank corners, equipment, and odd-looking spaces. Low-growing species should be placed near the front. Of course, you can vary the design endlessly as you like.

It always helps to have the driftwood or rocks in place first. Plant around and behind them to simulate a real underwater scene.

> **TIP**
>
> I recommend using only two or three types of plants in smaller tanks, as this will result in the most natural appearance. Larger tanks, obviously, offer more leeway in aquascaping.

Popular Plants for the Betta Tank

The plants described here are popular aquarium plants that will enhance your Betta tank. Some require specific lighting or water conditions to thrive, but others will adapt to almost any tank.

Anacharis are easy to care for, which makes them popular aquarium plants.

Anacharis *(Elodea densa)*

Anacharis is probably the most commonly kept aquarium plant, because it is hardy and easy to maintain. It can be kept as either floating plants or as rooted plants. Anacharis are great beginner plants because they adapt very easily, grow quickly, and are easily propagated. They are also good oxygenators. The stems will grow up to 20 inches or more, so they usually need to be kept trimmed.

Amazon Swords *(Echinodorus,* various species*)*

Several species collectively known as Amazon sword plants (shown on the first page of this chapter) can be found in aquarium shops. They have broad, sword or heart-shaped, coarse leaves on sturdy stems. Most grow more than a foot tall and will even bloom above the water surface in a large, brightly lit aquarium. They need plenty of sun and are poor choices for small tanks.

TIP

When aquascaping, place plants that require more light in higher locations and use taller species to hide filters and other equipment. To create a pleasing appearance, plant similar species in groups instead of sporadically, use rocks to accent plants, and place specimens with brightly colored leaves in prominent areas.

One, known in the trade as the pygmy sword plant, remains small and grasslike. With plenty of light it will carpet the bottom and create an extremely attractive display.

Arrowhead (*Sagittaria*, various species)

With broad to narrow, straplike underwater leaves, arrowhead grows naturally in tropical to temperate habitats. The name comes from the shape of the leaves that emerge from the water surface in natural ponds. Like sword plants, arrowheads need bright light and plenty of room. They can reach 3 feet or more in height. Most do poorly in acidic aquarium water, developing thin, brown spots on the leaves.

Crypts (*Cryptocoryne*, various species)

Among the best plants for a small aquarium, the numerous species of crypts live in shallow, warm waters like those inhabited by the Betta. Cousins of the common houseplant philodendron, crypts tolerate lower light levels than many other aquatic plants. Many have colorful foliage, and some readily produce side shoots that can be detached and replanted individually. Some will even bloom, producing flowers similar to a calla lily, when conditions are right.

Eelgrasses (*Vallisneria*, various species)

The hardy and fast-growing eelgrass species thrive in all kinds of water conditions and do not require intense lighting to reach maximum growth potential. They are perfect plants for the Betta aquarium and the beginning hobbyist. All have thin, elongated leaves that look like green fettuccine. All spread by means of short runners and can form a luxuriant stand when conditions are optimal.

Giant varieties grow 2 feet or more tall and look beautiful in a large tank. The most common ones are corkscrew types, in which the leaves spiral upward attractively. Corkscrew tiger eelgrass has dark and light variegations on the leaves, making it quite decorative.

Hornwort (*Ceratophyllum demersum*)

Hornwort is a floating, vinelike plant that seldom produces roots. The leaves are needlelike, arranged in whorls around the stem. Hornwort grows readily under

This is corkscrew eelgrass.

a variety of conditions, but will become stringy and lose leaves if the lighting is insufficient.

Hygro (*Hygrophila,* various species)

The Southeast Asian hygro family includes some truly hardy plants. The oval, pointed leaves grow in pairs on either side of the stem. If you provide this species with intense light, the foliage will become denser. This plant thrives in a Betta aquarium and is not difficult to maintain. (See photo on page 72.)

Java Fern *(Microsorium pteropus)*

Java fern has large leaves that form a point at the top. It requires moderate lighting conditions. Plants should be attached to a piece of driftwood, as described earlier in this chapter. (See photo on page 73.)

Hygro thrives in good light.

Java fern needs to be anchored in the tank.

Water Lettuce (*Pistia stratiodes*)

Water lettuce is a popular floating plant with long, dangling roots. Its leaves provide shade and the roots shelter small fish. It needs plenty of light. Because the leaves can grow upright as much as 6 inches tall, you may need to lower the water level in the tank to accommodate water lettuce.

Water Lilies (*Nymphaea*, various species)

The water lilies seen in garden ponds get far too large and require far too much sun to do well in most Betta aquariums. However, dwarf varieties can sometimes be found in aquarium shops and make an excellent centerpiece for the Betta tank. The long stems, often purplish in color or with attractive mottling, lift the thin, arrowhead-shaped floating leaves a foot or more to the surface. Well-grown plants will produce their lovely fragrant flowers, looking like miniature versions of garden pond lilies.

Water Sprite (*Ceratopteris,* various species)

An aquatic fern, water sprite produces thin, lobed, pale green leaves and does well in moderately lit, slightly acidic water. Offspring are produced in the notches between the leaf lobes. When they develop enough roots, the little plantlets can be detached and rooted in the substrate, or allowed to float like water lettuce. Snails will destroy this plant quickly if they get into your aquarium.

Water sprite can be rooted or left to float.

Keeping Plants Healthy

Just like houseplants, aquarium plants need regular care to keep them healthy. Be sure to always trim any dead leaves from the plant before they start to rot and foul your aquarium.

Temperature   Tropical aquarium plants grow well within the same temperature range required by the fish.

Plant Foods   A variety of plant foods are available from your local aquarium dealer. Tablets and liquid feeders can be placed in the gravel near the plants' roots. Special fertilizer "plugs" can be purchased that will provide nutrition for your plants continuously. A single cutting can be placed in the center of each plug and then buried as a whole unit in the gravel. Some hobbyists swear by a claylike material placed in a layer under the substrate. Just remember not to overdo the feedings or you will end up with a tank full of algae instead of thriving plants.

Lighting   Aquarium plants need at least eight hours of light per day to ensure good health; twelve hours of light is better. Planted tanks generally require more intense lighting than tanks that have only fish, so choose your lighting system appropriately. As a general rule, provide two or more fluorescent tubes that are as long as the tank itself. For a 24-inch tank, this means two 20-watt fluorescent lamps.

The table below provides lighting guidelines for common tank sizes.

Tank Size	Watts × No. of Lamps	Hours per Day
20 gallons	20 × 2	12
30 gallons	30 × 2	12
55 gallons	40 × 2	12
75 gallons	40 × 4	12

Water Conditions   Aquarium plants need the same water conditions that aquarium fish require. They also need water that is free of particulate debris, because cloudy water inhibits light penetration. Also, debris will settle on the surface of the leaves, shading them and looking unsightly.

Chapter 7

Bringing Your Betta Home

You'll need to get your aquarium system running before you bring any fish home. Let it run a day or two so you're sure everything works properly. Now you're ready to add some fish. Having a happy, healthy Betta depends upon finding a top quality specimen at your aquarium dealer.

Choosing the Right Dealer

Building a personal relationship with a good a tropical fish dealer has many benefits. The best aquarium shops provide both good advice and comprehensive, customer-friendly service. A merchant who knows your name, your aquarium interests, your fish preferences, and your aquarium specifications is well-equipped to help you become a successful hobbyist.

Visit as many local dealers as your time and budget will allow. Do the shop's employees greet you in a friendly manner? Do they offer good advice? Do they take an interest in your personal aquarium project and try to make sure you find exactly what you are looking for? Are there enough personnel, especially during peak hours?

Take the time to inspect all of the livestock display aquariums. Are the dealer's tanks clean and well maintained? More than anything else, tanks full of healthy, active fish distinguish a good dealer from an uncaring merchant. A quality dealer will make sure their establishment makes the best presentation possible.

Next, check out the fish. Do they swim without effort near the top of the tank, or do they hide in corners? Do all the fish appear to be in good health?

The Qualities of a Good Dealer

A good tropical fish dealer will greet you pleasantly and will always ask if you need help. Good dealers will also help you understand equipment and aquarium basics, discuss the pros and cons of your selections, refuse to sell you fish that are not compatible, and have clean display tanks with healthy fish.

Healthy fish hold their fins erect. They swim normally, searching for food. Their coloration appears normal for the species.

When your final selection has been made, make an effort to become well acquainted with each worker in the shop. Good dealers enjoy "talking tanks" with repeat customers. Over a period of time, a good dealer will become almost as familiar with your tank as you are. Caring merchants proudly share their customers' successes and sympathize with their failures, such as your Betta spawning or the loss of a favorite fish.

How to Pick a Healthy Fish

Choosing healthy tropical fish requires a combination of knowledge and common sense. Most people would reject a fish with an obvious wound, for example. When selecting new acquisitions for your home aquarium, follow a few simple rules.

Avoid buying new arrivals that your dealer has recently received from the shipper. A caring dealer will recommend that you wait until the fish have undergone a quarantine period before you take one home. Most dealers are happy to hold new arrivals for a week or so if you've committed to purchasing a certain fish. Some may require a reasonable deposit.

If, upon closer inspection, you find a dead fish in an apparently healthy tank, avoid buying livestock from that particular aquarium. Come back a week later and re-inspect this tank carefully. Fish sometimes die despite the best care, but you want to make sure this was the case, and not an outbreak of a contagious disease.

Do not purchase "humpbacked" Bettas, because this physical trait is generally an indication of old age. A good dealer would not display fish in this condition.

A healthy Betta will have a deep, rich body color and no scars, wounds, tears, or sores.

The box on page 79 describes the characteristics of a healthy Betta. If the apparent health of the fish does not meet the criteria listed, it is better to exercise a little patience and wait for healthier fish to arrive before making a purchase. When it comes to fish healthcare, avoiding problems always meets with greater success than trying to cure them.

Until you gain some experience with tropical aquariums, avoid hard-to-maintain species and unfamiliar fish. As you browse through the shop looking for tankmates for your Betta, write down the names of all the fish that appeal to you. Discuss your selections with your dealer. Ask which species are compatible with your Betta, and which are hardy and do not have difficult or unique dietary requirements. Shops always have dozens of easy, hardy community fish. Leave the more demanding species to the experts.

How Many Is Too Many?

Before you buy any fish for your new aquarium, it is essential to calculate the total number of fish (your Betta and its tankmates) that can be safely housed in your tank. The maximum number that can be kept safely within your aquarium tank is known as the carrying capacity.

Overstocking is probably the most common error made by beginning hobbyists. You must be consciously aware of your aquarium's carrying capacity. The old rule was "1 inch of fish per gallon," but that formula has serious limitations. In fact, the weight of the fish, not its length, determines its food and energy needs. Weighing fish is impractical, but if we designate a "standard" fish, we can arrive at an estimate of carrying capacity based on your tank's surface area.

The Healthy Betta

Physical Characteristics

Look for the following traits in the fish when you shop:

- Deep, rich body colors
- No visible ulcers, boils, or skin problems
- No visible scars or wounds
- Long and flowing, or short and erect fins; not fins that are ragged, torn, missing, collapsed, or clamped close to the body
- Flat, smooth scales, not protruding from the body
- Well rounded stomach, but no swelling in the abdominal area
- Body of normal girth, neither bloated nor emaciated
- Visible excreta (fish waste) that is dark, not colorless
- Clear eyes, neither clouded nor protruding from the sockets
- No visible external parasites, such as ich (small white dots) or velvet (a dusty gold mist)

Tank Habits

A healthy Betta will:

- Swim horizontally, with its head neither elevated nor lowered
- Swim without effort
- Swim throughout the entire length of the aquarium, not lurk in corners or hide behind decorations
- Breathe normally, not heave rapidly or gulp for air

For our standard fish, we will use the Zebra Danio *(Brachydanio rerio)*. Sure to be found in nearly any aquarium shop, the Zebra Danio swims most of the time, has a typical fish shape, and grows to about 2 inches long. Experience has shown that an adult Danio needs about half a square foot of surface area in the aquarium. That gives us our crucial ratio: 2 inches of "standard" fish per one-half square foot, or 4 inches of fish per square foot. Let's plug these numbers into our earlier example of a 20-gallon tank:

Tank width: 12 inches (1 foot)

Tank length: 24 inches (2 feet)

First, you must multiply the tank width by the tank length to get the total number of square feet:

1 foot × 2 feet = 2 square feet

Next, multiply the result by 4 (because you can have 4 inches of fish per square foot):

2 square feet × 4 inches of fish = 8 inches

So, an aquarium measuring 12 inches by 24 inches can safely keep four adult Zebra Danios, each 2 inches long in adulthood. Or one male Betta (which is 3 inches long) and three, maybe four, Zebra Danios. The Betta swims more languidly than the frenetic Danios, so I'd go with four because the lower activity level of the Betta "leaves room" for additional Danios. Making choices like this becomes easier with experience. At first, rely on your dealer for recommendations and remember the formula above. Always start with fewer fish. You can add more later.

Fish dealers generally bend the rules for stocking limits because they use high-capacity equipment to filter and aerate their display tanks. You won't be

Guppies are about 2 inches long, which means you can add two of them per square foot of surface area in your aquarium.

> ### Transporting Your Betta
>
> Here are some handy tips for transporting your Betta home.
>
> - Ask the dealer if they can add pure oxygen to the fish's bag.
> - Don't run errands after buying your fish—bring it directly home.
> - Turn the bag upside down in the carrier so there are no corners to trap the Betta.
> - Use an insulated container for transport to minimize temperature fluctuations.

able to do the same at home, unless you are committed to a professional-quality filtration system and daily maintenance. Be sure to provide enough space for each fish so that your new pets won't be stressed out before they have even had a chance to become acclimated to their new home.

The Trip Home

When you move your Betta from a dealer's tank to your home aquarium, you must take steps to minimize the shock of transport so that your fish will have the best possible chance of survival.

Make sure that the dealer packs your new Betta properly. For example, just a little bit of extra water in the bag can greatly reduce stress and make all the difference in the world.

I firmly believe that all fish should be double bagged as a hedge against leaks. If a shipping bag is flawed or becomes damaged in packing, it may leak during your trip. Using double bags as a safety measure is just good common sense.

The shipping bags should be dark in color to help calm your Betta and its tankmates during transport. If your dealer uses clear bags (most do), make sure you put them in a paper bag or box for transport. I like to carry a small picnic cooler in the trunk of my car for this purpose. Not only does it provide darkness, but the insulation helps keep the bag at the proper temperature. You can also use a cardboard box, and packing material such as Styrofoam peanuts can be used to absorb shocks and minimize temperature swings.

New Tank Syndrome

"New tank syndrome" sometimes develops while the tank is going through the conditioning period (see chapter 5, "Ready for Setup"). The beneficial bacteria need time to adjust to each addition of fish. Add too many fish too soon and ammonia will be produced faster than the bacteria can deal with it. The resulting rise in ammonia may stress your new aquatic pets to the point that disease develops. Too much ammonia will result in death.

Fish that are suffering from the ill effects of new tank syndrome will often be pale in color, have clamped fins, hang near the bottom of the tank, and hide behind decorations. If you notice any unusual behaviors after adding new fish, test the ammonia and nitrite levels of your water immediately. If you find either one is too high, do a partial water change to lower the levels. You may need to keep doing partial water changes every few days until tests show the tank has stabilized.

To be safe, add only one or two small fish per week to the aquarium. Gradually increasing the tank's population usually holds ammonia levels within a minimum range.

During the first week after setup, the water may become cloudy. Don't panic! The cloudiness results from a bloom of bacterial growth, including the beneficial nitrifying bacteria. Just be patient; the water should become clear again after the tank has been running for a week or two.

Add new fish gradually, giving the ecosystem in the tank time to adjust.

Quarantining New Fish

Maintaining a simple quarantine tank may not be fun, but it is truly the best way to get your hobby off to a good start. By quarantining each new arrival, you can greatly reduce the possibility of a disease outbreak in your main display aquarium. Because of the stresses of capture and transport, new fish are always more susceptible to problems than healthy fish that are already established in the aquarium. Adding a new fish without quarantining it may create two problems. First, ammonia may increase slightly as the bacteria gear up for the new arrival's impact. This may stress both new and established fish. Second, the new fish can be a source of disease organisms. The combination of stress and a source of infection can be deadly to all concerned.

The quarantine tank can be simple, and needs only to be large enough for the largest fish you contemplate adding to your display tank. For most people, a 20-gallon tank with a hang-on power filter, a thin layer of substrate, and a good heater are all that's required. To provide hiding places, pick up a few PVC pipe couplings at your nearest home improvement store. The ones made for 2-inch drain pipe are perfect for sheltering most small tropical fish, are easily disinfected after use, and cost about a dollar apiece. Set up the tank as you would a display tank, and have it ready a few days before you buy the first fish.

> ### T I P
>
> **New Fish**
>
> Before adding new fish to your tank, turn off all aquarium lights. Allow the temperature to equalize before you release the new fish. After release, watch the tank carefully for at least an hour while the new inhabitants become accustomed to their surroundings and tankmates.

Into the Tank

Moving a fish from a shipping bag into the tank, whether for quarantine or display, should be done with care. First, turn off all aquarium lights so that your new arrival will not be harassed by established tankmates (if there are any). The comforting darkness will also help to reduce stress.

It's likely that the temperature of the water in your fish's bag will be different from the water in the tank. To avoid a sudden change in temperature, open the top of the bag and float it in the aquarium for fifteen minutes as you add tank water to it in small amounts every few minutes. This will help to equalize the temperature. Finally, carefully tip the bag forward and allow your new fish to swim out on its own.

Betta

2nd Edition

John H. Tullock

Howell
Book House™

Copyright © 2006 by Wiley Publishing, Inc., Hoboken, New Jersey. All rights reserved.

Photos © Aaron Norman.

Howell Book House
Published by Wiley Publishing, Inc., Hoboken, New Jersey

The publisher and the author make no representations or warranties with respect to the accuracy or completeness of the contents of this work and specifically disclaim all warranties, including without limitation warranties of fitness for a particular purpose. No warranty may be created or extended by sales or promotional materials. The advice and strategies contained herein may not be suitable for every situation. This work is sold with the understanding that the publisher is not engaged in rendering legal, accounting, or other professional services. If professional assistance is required, the services of a competent professional person should be sought. Neither the publisher nor the author shall be liable for damages arising here from. The fact that an organization or Website is referred to in this work as a citation and/or a potential source of further information does not mean that the author or the publisher endorses the information the organization or Website may provide or recommendations it may make. Further, readers should be aware that Internet Websites listed in this work may have changed or disappeared between when this work was written and when it is read.

For general information on our other products and services or to obtain technical support please contact our Customer Care Department within the U.S. at (800) 762-2974, outside the U.S. at (317) 572-3993 or fax (317) 572-4002.

Wiley also publishes its books in a variety of electronic formats. Some content that appears in print may not be available in electronic books. For more information about Wiley products, please visit our web site at www.wiley.com.

Library of Congress Cataloging-in-Publication Data:
Tullock, John H., 1951-
Betta/John Tullock.—2nd ed.
 p. cm.—(Your happy healthy pet)
 ISBN-13: 978-0-471-79380-9 (cloth: alk. paper)
 ISBN-10: 0-471-79380-9 (alk. paper)
 1. Betta. 2. Aquarium fishes. I. Title. II. Series.
 SF458.B4T85 2006
 639.3'77—dc22   2006003801

Printed in the United States of America
10 9 8 7 6 5 4 3 2 1
2nd Edition

Book design by Melissa Auciello-Brogan
Cover design by Michael J. Freeland
Book production by Wiley Publishing, Inc. Composition Services

About the Author

John H. Tullock has been keeping tropical fish since he was 8 years old. His *Natural Reef Aquariums* has been required reading for saltwater hobbyists since it was first published in 1997. His other aquarium books include *The Reef Tank Owner's Manual, Successful Saltwater Aquariums, Your First Marine Aquarium, Clownfish and Sea Anemones, Corals, A Dictionary of Aquarium Terms,* and *Water Chemistry for the Marine Aquarium*. In addition, hundreds of his articles about aquarium-keeping have appeared in magazines since 1980.

Tullock holds a master's degree in biology. He is the founder of the American Marinelife Dealers Association, an organization dedicated to environmentally sound aquarium keeping. He was a member of the steering committee that created the Marine Aquarium Council. He serves on the board of directors of Conservation Fisheries, a nonprofit organization that raises rare and endangered North American fishes for recovery programs, and is a member of the board of advisors of Reef Protection International.

Also an avid gardener and photographer, Tullock's most recent book is *Growing Hardy Orchids* (Timber Press).

About Howell Book House

Since 1961, Howell Book House has been America's premier publisher of pet books. We're dedicated to companion animals and the people who love them, and our books reflect that commitment. Our stable of authors—training experts, veterinarians, breeders, and other authorities—is second to none. And we've won more Maxwell Awards from the Dog Writers Association of America than any other publisher.

As we head toward the half-century mark, we're more committed than ever to providing new and innovative books, along with the classics our readers have grown to love. This year, we're launching several exciting new initiatives, including redesigning the Howell Book House logo and revamping our biggest pet series, Your Happy Healthy Pet™, with bold new covers and updated content. From bringing home a new puppy to competing in advanced equestrian events, Howell has the titles that keep animal lovers coming back again and again.

Contents

Part I: All About Bettas   8

Chapter 1: The Jewel of the Orient   11
The Betta Family   12
A History of Betta Keeping   13
Betta Fighting   13
A Suitable Environment   15

Chapter 2: Betta Basics   17
What Is a Betta?   17
Body Functions   22
A Betta's Senses   23
The Labyrinth Organ   25

Chapter 3: Bettas and Their Tankmates   27
Varieties of Bettas   27
Betta Color Patterns   33
Tankmates for Bettas   34

Part II: Setting Up the Aquarium   38

Chapter 4: Understanding Aquarium Equipment   40
Things to Think About   40
Tank Types   43
Substrate   46
Filtration Systems   47
Three Types of Filtration   48
Heaters   51
Lighting   52
Other Equipment   54

Chapter 5: Ready for Setup   56
The Stand and Tank   56
Decorations   58
Aeration   60
Water Quality   61
The Nitrogen Cycle   63
Adding Fish   65

Chapter 6: Plants for the Betta Tank   66
Purchasing Plants   66
Aquascaping   68
Popular Plants for the Betta Tank   68
Keeping Plants Healthy   75

Chapter 7: Bringing Your Betta Home   **76**

Choosing the Right Dealer   76
How to Pick a Healthy Fish   77
How Many Is Too Many?   78
The Healthy Betta   79
The Trip Home   81
New Tank Syndrome   82
Quarantining New Fish   83
Into the Tank   83

Part III: Keeping Your Betta Healthy and Happy   **84**

Chapter 8: Feeding Your Betta   **86**

A Betta's Nutritional Needs   86
Feeding Schedule   87
A Varied Diet   88
Algae   90
Appetite Loss   91

Chapter 9: Healthy Tank, Healthy Fish   **92**

Examining Your Fish   92
Maintaining a Healthy Tank   94
Common Illnesses   94
A Quick Reference Guide to Diseases   100
Other Causes of Disease   102
A Hospital Tank   103
Treatment Tips   104

Chapter 10: Breeding Your Bettas   **107**

Mouthbrooders   107
Nest Builders   108
The Breeding Room   109
Selecting Breeding Stock   109
Setting Up a Breeding Tank   110
Conditioning Breeders   112
Introducing Bettas to the Breeding Tank   114
Spawning Rituals   116
Caring for the Eggs   118
Caring for the Fry   118

Appendix: Learning More About Your Betta   **121**

Books   121
Magazines   122
Internet Resources   123
Clubs and Organizations   124

Index   **125**

Shopping List

You'll need to do a bit of stocking up before you bring your fish home. Below is a basic list of some must-have supplies. For more detailed information on selecting each item below, consult chapters 4 and 5. For specific guidance on what fish food you'll need, review chapter 8.

- ☐ Tank
- ☐ Tank stand
- ☐ Aquarium hood
- ☐ Filter
- ☐ Water quality test kit
- ☐ Air pump
- ☐ Airstones
- ☐ Air hose
- ☐ Heater
- ☐ Thermometer

- ☐ Aquarium light
- ☐ Gravel
- ☐ Plants
- ☐ Algae scraper
- ☐ Aquarium vacuum
- ☐ Nets
- ☐ 5-gallon bucket
- ☐ Siphon hose
- ☐ Fish food

There are likely to be a few other items that you're dying to pick up before bringing your fish home. Use the following blanks to note any additional items you'll be shopping for.

- ☐ _____
- ☐ _____
- ☐ _____
- ☐ _____
- ☐ _____
- ☐ _____
- ☐ _____
- ☐ _____

Pet Sitter's Guide

We can be reached at ( ) ___-_____ Cellphone ( ) ___- _____

We will return on _____ (date) at _____ (approximate time)

Other individual to contact in case of emergency _____

Number of fish we have _____

Care Instructions

In the following sections let the sitter know what to feed, how much, and when; what tasks need to be performed daily; and what weekly tasks they'll be responsible for.

Morning _____

_____

_____

_____

_____

_____

Evening _____

_____

_____

_____

_____

_____

Other tasks and special instructions _____

_____

_____

_____

_____

_____

_____

_____

_____

_____

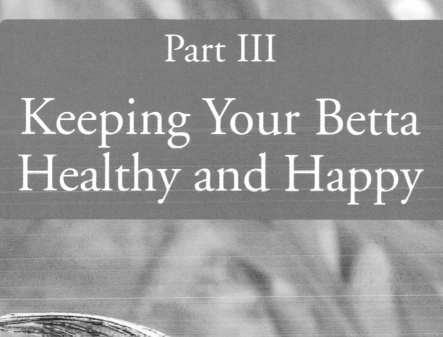

Part III

Keeping Your Betta Healthy and Happy

Chapter 8

Feeding Your Betta

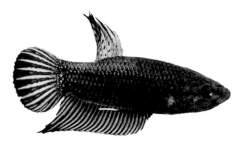

If you want your Betta and its tankmates to grow strong and healthy and show good coloration, you will need to give your fish a proper diet. Good nutrition is really not as confusing as you might think. Commercial aquarium foods provide all the nutrients your fish require for good health. Feeding a variety of flake, frozen, fresh, and live foods keeps fish healthy, brightly colored, and active.

In the wild, Bettas mainly eat insects that fall into the water. In the home aquarium, the proteins, fats, vitamins, fiber, and carbohydrates that are normally obtained in their natural diet must be provided by you. A well-fed Betta will be less likely to contract a disease than a poorly fed one.

A Betta's Nutritional Needs

With a little knowledge of fundamental nutritional principles, you will quickly gain a better understanding of how to feed your Betta properly.

- **Vitamins** help make the body tissues resilient to disease. They also help to combat eye problems, skin hemorrhages, and anemia. Vitamins may be lost from foods during processing, so live and frozen foods provide the best sources. You can also add a vitamin supplement to processed foods such as flake foods. Ask your dealer about vitamin supplements if they do not stock live foods.
- **Minerals** play many roles in maintaining your Betta's health. They are important in bone formation and fluid regulation. Prepared foods containing algae or seaweed provide minerals, and many manufacturers

supplement flake foods with minerals. As with vitamins, the best approach is to feed a variety of foods.

- **Proteins** provide energy and help your Betta build strong muscle and body tissue. Thus, proteins are essential for growth. Younger fish need more protein than adults. Live foods such as brine shrimp and blackworms supply plenty of protein, as do frozen foods and flakes. Look for foods made specifically for fish that eat animal protein, usually labeled for "carnivorous" fish.

- **Carbohydrates** provide energy for your Betta and help it resist disease, but they may be harmful in excessive levels. Most foods will provide sufficient carbohydrates, so you needn't worry too much about this class of nutrients.

> **T I P**
>
> **High-Protein Foods**
>
> Here are some high-protein foods to supplement your Betta's diet.
>
> Baby guppies
>
> Frozen seafoods
>
> Insects
>
> Worms

Feeding Schedule

Bettas need frequent, small meals. Most hobbyists find that scheduling feedings in the morning and evening works best. If you have the time to feed your fish more frequently, do so, but take care to keep the servings small. For a twice daily schedule, feed what the fish will eat in ten minutes. For more frequent feedings, cut that amount in half. As the aquarium matures, especially if live plants are present, tiny invertebrates and algae will grow naturally. The fish will feed on these organisms, supplementing the food you provide.

Bettas and their tankmates may literally beg for food by swimming up to the surface and imitating a starving animal. Avoid the temptation to toss in a pinch of food every time these moochers look hungry or distressed; you will only overfeed them. Establish a feeding schedule and stick to it.

Bettas are not aggressive feeders and will often hang back while other fish greedily devour every bit of food that is put into the aquarium. If your Betta has other tankmates, pay attention to the social situation at feeding time. If aggressive fish get all the goodies, you may need to remove them. Choosing tankmates carefully usually avoids this problem.

Bettas do best on a regular feeding schedule.

A Varied Diet

Would you like to eat meatloaf every day for a year? Bettas have been known to stop eating entirely when offered only one type of food for a long period of time. This is not a symptom of boredom, but rather of extreme stress. Fish stop eating only when things have gone very wrong. In this case, malnutrition and dietary deficiencies are the culprits. These conditions may cause damage to the internal organs, nerves, or body chemistry that is not apparent until the problem becomes severe.

Many types of foods stocked by your dealer can be combined to form a proper diet for your Betta. These include live brine shrimp, dry flake food, worms, freeze-dried products (algae, *Daphnia,* krill) and frozen foods. Feeding a variety of foods ensures that your Betta will receive healthy, balanced nutrition.

Flake Foods

Flake foods will provide a staple diet for your Betta and its tankmates. Flakes will float at the water's surface and then sink as they become saturated. Tropical fish flakes usually combine ingredients such as fish meal, wheat flour, shrimp meal, fish protein, egg, oil, vitamin supplements, and minerals.

Purchase flake foods with the idea of using them within six months. Discard any that develop a musty or moldy smell.

Pellet Foods

Pellet foods are designed to either float or sink. Floating pellets provide good nutrition for surface feeders, but may be too large for your Betta to consume easily. Sinking pellets are perfect for any bottom-dwelling inhabitants, such as Catfish, that share your Betta's home.

Frozen Foods

Commercial fish food is available in a variety of forms. Flakes are especially good for Bettas.

Frozen foods may contain only vegetables; others may use a variety of meats and other animal proteins as the main ingredients. By alternating your purchases of frozen foods among various types, you will be able to supply your Betta with many interesting and nutritious meals.

Keep frozen food solidly frozen until you are ready to use it. Foods such as brine shrimp will spoil quickly once thawed. Never refreeze any frozen foods after they have thawed. Treat frozen fish foods as you would food for human consumption.

Bettas Love Mosquito Larvae

One of the Betta's natural foods is mosquito larvae. In some parts of the country, you can easily obtain them by leaving a plastic dish pan half full of water in a shady spot. Check the pan every day for "wigglers." Harvest the larvae by pouring the contents of the pan through a small net, rinse briefly under the tap, and feed the little critters to your aquarium fish. Refill the dish pan to raise another "crop."

Obviously, you should not place the pan in an area where biting adult mosquitoes might create a problem. And don't allow the larvae to mature. They can transform into hungry adults in a matter of days. Feed them to the fish, dump the pan, and start over.

Freeze-Dried Foods

Freeze-dried foods contain no moisture and can be stored for long periods. Most of the standard frozen foods are also available in freeze-dried form. They will stay fresh as long as they are stored in an area free from excessive heat and moisture. Always soak freeze-dried food in water before using it. Soaking restores some of the texture, making the food easier to eat. Freeze-dried foods expand when wet; always base the portion size on rehydrated food. Adding this food to the aquarium when it is dry will result in overfeeding.

Live Food

Despite the fact that they are in a captive environment, Bettas still enjoy hunting live food when it is provided. Live aquarium foods should be purchased from your dealer or cultivated in your basement or garage. Collecting live foods from the wild, once a weekend excursion for many dedicated aquarists, now poses risks of introducing disease and unwanted pests.

Your Bettas will enjoy live blackworms, small, semi-aquatic relatives of the earthworm that are cultured and sold for fish food. Keep them in the refrigerator in a shallow container, covered with about half an inch of water. Change the water daily and they will keep for a month.

Live adult brine shrimp also make great Betta food. Dealers bring them in from growers in Florida and sell small portions. A portion only keeps for a few days, so feed them promptly. You can also raise baby brine shrimp from eggs. Purchase a small vial of eggs at the aquarium dealer and follow the label instructions to hatch them in an empty mayonnaise jar. Virtually all tropical fish love brine shrimp and watching "the hunt" is fun.

> **TIP**
>
> **Earthworms**
>
> Bait shops sell earthworms. Your Betta and its tankmates will love them as a special treat. Keep the earthworms in a cool place and they will last several weeks. Remove one or two worms from the carton and rinse in an old kitchen strainer. Chop into pieces for your fish.

Algae

Research has shown that green algae benefits tropical fish by providing them with the vitamins and nutrients needed for good health and outstanding color. In a well-lit tank, algae will inevitably grow on the glass. It can be quickly and easily removed with an algae scraper. Algae growing on top of rocks and plant leaves can be left

Overfeeding

One of the main rules of aquatic nutrition is don't overfeed. Your Betta's stomach is not much larger than the size of its eye. It does not take vast amounts of food to keep your pet full. Continual overfeeding will foul the water, which can lead to disease problems. If you entrust someone to feed the tank while you are away, place a day's portion of food in a snack bag with instructions for your tank sitter. Weekly water changes and removing accumulated debris helps compensate for small excesses in feeding.

there for your aquatic pets to graze on. After the algae has grown into a healthy crop, you will notice that all your fish will continually feed upon this natural food, and it will prolong their lives and bolster their health.

Unsightly brown algae may grow if your lighting is insufficient. Clean brown algae off the glass and change the fluorescent lamp. If you already have a new lamp, add another one. Soon the algae growth will be green.

The algae on these rocks make a nutritious snack for your Betta.

Appetite Loss

Sometimes, a Betta simply stops eating. Polluted water, disease, old age, or harassment by other fish may be to blame.

Suspect one of these causes and take appropriate corrective action if your fish suddenly stops eating. Water tests will quickly indicate if there is ammonia pollution. Observe all fish for signs of disease, such as the tiny white dots indicating ich parasites. Harassment may not be obvious right away; watch the fish interact over a long period.

Of course, not much can be done about old age. But if your Betta has been with you long enough to show signs of advancing age, congratulations—you have been doing your job as an aquarist.

Chapter 9

Healthy Tank, Healthy Fish

Stress, poor diet, incorrect water conditions, and incompatible tankmates can all increase your Betta's chances of disease. By taking on the challenge of keeping a Betta in your home aquarium, you accept responsibility to give each of your wet pets the best possible care. After all, your Betta and its tankmates will give you years of enjoyment and relaxation. You owe them the same.

An aquarium offers other benefits as well. Researchers have found that people who keep aquariums generally have lower levels of physical and emotional stress. Individuals who reduce their daily load of stress may live longer lives. So your tropical fish can actually help you live a healthier life. You should return the favor by keeping them in prime condition by following good aquarium care techniques.

Examining Your Fish

Each day, carefully check the health of your fish. Is your Betta swimming normally or is it consistently lurking in corners? Are its eyes bright and alert or are they clouded over? Are your Betta's fins erect or clamped shut and drooping? Is its spine straight or curved? Does the body have normal, well-rounded proportions or is the stomach swollen or sunken?

Any clamped fins, shimmy, loss of appetite, paling or darkening of colors, increased respiration, or other abnormal behavior is a warning sign that disease or environmental conditions may have taken a turn for the worse. The importance of regularly observing your aquarium and all its inhabitants cannot be overemphasized.

Your Betta's fins should be flowing and undamaged.

Know Your Betta's Habits

Part of being a good fishkeeper is learning how to recognize unnatural behaviors. If your Betta is acting strangely, chances are there is a problem somewhere in your aquarium. Being able to identify odd behavior is the first step in disease prevention. The following list of abnormal Betta behaviors will alert you to a potential problem:

- Scratching itself on tank decorations or gravel
- Normally active but now moving slowly or not at all
- Floating upside down or swimming sideways
- Floating to the top or struggling to rise from the gravel
- Bloating or swelling on any body part
- Refusing to eat
- Visible damage to fins, eyes, or scales
- Spots or patches of abnormal or missing coloration
- Hanging around the heater all day
- Fins continuously clamped tightly against the body

If you notice any of these problems, check your aquarium conditions immediately.

Maintaining a Healthy Tank

How to keep your Betta happy and healthy is no secret. All you need to do is follow a few simple rules and keep a sharp eye out for problems. Check on your Betta's health at the same time you check the aquarium conditions: each and every day. If you constantly keep abreast of the conditions in your tank, you will be able to quickly correct any problems that may manifest.

Daily

Obviously, all equipment must be functioning properly. Check to make sure. Tubing sometimes clogs, and pumps wear out. Pay attention that flow rates appear normal.

Check the water temperature. Any fluctuation in temperature of more than 2 degrees from normal can quickly cause a health problem. If the temperature is wrong, check to make sure your heater is not stuck in either the on or off position. Replace a faulty heater immediately.

Incoming sunlight may cause overheating. Adding shades or blinds to a nearby window is a simple solution.

A failed air pump can usually be rebuilt by replacing worn diaphragms with packaged rebuild parts; these parts can be found at your local aquarium dealer or ordered online.

Every morning, take a quick inventory of all the fish. Remove dead fish immediately. If any seem to be ill, transfer them to your quarantine tank and begin treatment immediately. Quick action can help keep disease from spreading to other individuals.

Weekly

I recommend that you perform at least a 10-percent water change every week. Rainfall and runoff constantly cleanse and replace water in the Betta's natural environment. Plant growth and other natural processes remove pollutants. Wind creates turbulence that facilitates gas exchange. Pretend the water in your aquarium is your own personal water supply for

Common Illnesses

Here's a list of common illnesses, together with general guidelines for identifying and treating them. Keep in mind that treatments may be detrimental to live plants and that not all fish can tolerate some medications. Check medication the day. Would you feel comfortable drinking it? Remember, your Betta has to *live* in it.

Every week, siphon off any debris that has accumulated on top of the substrate. Check pH and nitrate levels to make sure they are within the proper range required for your Betta. If not, modify your procedure by changing more water, or by doing more frequent changes.

If the nitrate levels are too high, the best remedy is a 20 percent water change every day until the levels return to normal. Try to identify and correct any problem that is causing the nitrate levels to rise, such as poor filtration, overfeeding, or overcrowding. Get help from your dealer or another knowledgeable aquarist if the problem seems intractable.

Clean excess algae growth from the glass. Algae can interfere with the view and shade your aquatic plants. Leave the growth on the back glass to provide veggie snacks for the fish.

Monthly

Clean all filter pads and other media by rinsing them in the water you remove for a regular water change. Do not use tap water for this task, as you will destroy beneficial bacteria. After several cycles of use, rinsing, and reuse, filter pads will need to be replaced. When the time comes, install the new pad but leave the old one sitting in the filter box to provide plenty of "seed" bacteria for the new pad. After a couple of weeks, toss the old pad.

Once or Twice a Year

Once or twice a year, your Betta's aquarium should experience a "thunderstorm." Stir up the gravel a bit, prune plants that have become rangy, siphon out all the debris, and change half the water. Replace the filter pads at the same time to collect more of the debris you've dislodged. A major cleaning simulates what happens in the Betta's natural habitat when a thunderstorm scours the area. You don't need to go to the extreme of breaking down the tank and uprooting all the plants. Just give everything a thorough going over and a big water change. When things settle down in a day or two, you'll be amazed at how vibrant your aquarium looks.

labels for any warnings from the manufacturer. If at all possible, carry out treatments in a quarantine tank. Adding a treatment to a display tank, with many different fish and plants, may do more harm than good. Of course, if every fish in the tank has ich, for example, you have no choice but to medicate the whole tank.

Stress and Other Factors

Most illnesses found in aquarium fish result from stress caused by poor environmental conditions. Disease organisms and parasites may lie dormant until the Betta has become weakened by fluctuating environmental factors. In the home aquarium, your Betta lives in an enclosed ecosystem that is vulnerable to imbalance. Given the relative stability of its native environment, the Betta's ability to adapt to change is limited.

If you do notice warning signs of illness, don't panic. Take time to check on the efficiency of the equipment, test the water conditions, and rule out other stress factors, such as harassment by other fish. Once you have analyzed all of this information, you will be able to make a sound decision about the proper course of action.

Bacterial Septicemia

Occurrence: Infrequent
Symptoms: Inflamed red streaks appear on the fins and body. Other symptoms include hemorrhages, listlessness, and refusal to eat. This disease usually occurs after a fish has been afflicted with fin rot or skin infections. Poor water conditions and low temperatures may leave fish susceptible.
Cause: *Pseudomonas* or *Streptococcus* bacteria
Treatment: Consult a veterinarian for antibiotic treatment, which must be carried out in a quarantine tank.

Constipation

Occurrence: Common
Symptoms: Poor appetite, swollen stomach region, inactivity, pale, stringy feces remain attached to the anus
Cause: Incorrect diet, overfeeding
Treatment: Fish should go without eating for several days. Then switch to live foods for awhile. Gradually switch back to prepared foods with occasional live treats, but strive to improve the diet. Check with your dealer for recommendations.

Any spot or patch that mars your fish's scales is a sign of trouble.

Dropsy

Occurrence: Rare
Symptoms: Swollen body, protruding scales, bloated eyes
Cause: Organ failure, probably from a variety of causes
Treatment: None, recovery is rare. Affected fish should be euthanized.

Fin Rot

Occurrence: Common
Symptoms: Inflamed rays; torn, ragged or disintegrating fins
Cause: Either poor water quality or fin injury from fighting can cause this disease, a bacterial infection that can erode the fins and tail all the way down to the body. A secondary fungal infection may accompany fin rot.
Treatment: Spot-treat infected areas with 50 percent mercurochrome, gentian violet, or methylene blue applied with a cotton swab. Add 1 tablespoon of aquarium salt for each 5 gallons of water to help with regulation of body fluids. Test the water and perform frequent water changes to maintain the best possible conditions.

Fish Lice

Occurrence: Infrequent
Symptoms: Disk-shaped parasites can be found attached to the skin of the Betta. Ulcers can be seen near the point of parasitic attachment. Bacteria or fungus may attack the resulting wound.

Cause: A crustacean parasite is the cause. After feeding on the skin, the adult parasite will leave its host and lay gelatinlike capsules full of eggs. Often the eggs will not hatch until the temperature rises and may stay in the tank for long periods of time. It is more of a problem in outdoor ponds and large holding systems than in home aquariums. Typically, a single parasite arrives unnoticed, attached to a fish. Prompt action in removing it prevents it from becoming established in the tank.

Treatment: Remove the parasite from the Betta with a small pair of tweezers. Dab any wounds using a cotton swab that has been dipped in 50 percent mercurochrome.

Fungus

Occurrence: Common

Symptoms: White, cottony growths on the body or fins

Cause: The growths occur in regions where the mucus or slime coating has been damaged by parasites or suffered injury. Most of the time, the cause is not a fungus but a bacterial infection. If the infection is severe, water molds, such as *Saprolegnia* and *Achyla*, may produce a secondary infection.

Treatment: Isolate the fish in a quarantine tank. Spot-treat with 50 percent mercurochrome, gentian violet, or methylene blue applied with a cotton swab directly to the injured area. Severe cases are usually untreatable.

By regularly observing your fish, you will be able to spot signs of trouble early on.

Gill Parasites

Occurrence: Infrequent
Symptoms: Labored respiration, scratching, glazed eyes, and loss of motor control
Cause: Flukes *(Dactylogyrus)*
Treatment: Consult a veterinarian.

Ich

Occurrence: Very common
Symptoms: Small white spots on the body or fins that resemble little grains of salt. Fish that are infected with ich will scratch themselves on gravel and decorations during the advanced stages of this disease. Without a doubt, ich causes more problems for aquarists than any of the other conditions described in this book.
Cause: Adult *Ichthyopthirius* parasites will fall off the host, sink to the bottom of the tank, and multiply in the gravel. New parasites will be released to find another host.
Treatment: Use a commercial ich remedy (formalin or malachite green). Ich does not need to be treated in a quarantine tank. The infectious nature of the parasite ensures other fish will be infected if the whole tank is not treated promptly.

Intestinal Parasites

Occurrence: Infrequent
Symptoms: Worms showing through the vent; emaciation
Cause: Different varieties of intestinal worms
Treatment: Veterinarian-prescribed anthelminthic should be given in the diet. Add 1 tablespoon of aquarium salt for every 5 gallons of water to help with regulation of body fluids. Remove any activated carbon from the filters. Change 10 percent of the water daily.

Mouth Fungus

Occurrence: Infrequent
Symptoms: Cottonlike growths around the mouth or patchy white skin
Cause: Usually a *Saprolegnia* species, often occurring after another infection has set in
Treatment: Commercial medications often contain methylene blue. This dye interferes with biological filtration and should be used only in a quarantine

A Quick Reference Guide to Diseases

Here's a quick guide for troubleshooting disease problems. Remember, a single symptom can be indicative of many different types of diseases. This table will provide you with a general pathway toward locating the correct problem.

Symptom	Possible Problem
Spots on skin	Ich; velvet
Slimy skin	Ich; velvet
Cottonlike growths	Fungus
Parasite visible	Anchor worm; fish lice
Ulcer visible	Bacterial infection; wound
Faded color	Stress
Bad equilibrium	Swim bladder disorder
Rapid breathing	Low oxygen; gill parasites
Erratic behavior	Polluted water
Convulsions	Poison; severe internal disease
Constant scratching	Parasites; poor water conditions
Weight loss	Stress; tuberculosis

tank. If over-the-counter treatments are not effective, consult your veterinarian about antibiotics.

Pop Eye

Occurrence: Infrequent

Symptoms: Inflamed eyes protruding from their sockets. Often the eyes will develop a white haze. Inflamed eye sockets are also common.

Cause: Infection, parasites, or poor environmental conditions

Treatment: The only thing that you can do to help your Betta overcome pop eye is to improve the aquarium's water conditions with frequent changes and add 1 tablespoon of aquarium salt per 5 gallons of water to help with regulation of body fluids. Check water conditions with test kits to ensure they remain within the correct range.

> ## Maintaining Your Betta's Slime Coat
>
> The Betta's slime coat prevents the loss of salts from the gills and skin. If large areas of the slime coat are lost, these salts will be depleted in your Betta's body. This loss can lead to a higher risk of disease and even cause heart failure.
>
> Avoid handling fish with nets to help protect the slime coat. Commercial products that claim to enhance the slime coat are widely available. However, your Betta's best slime coat protection comes from living in a properly maintained aquarium and eating a healthy, varied diet.

Slime Disease

Occurrence: Very common
Symptoms: A gray coating on the body or fins, scratching, frayed fins, and shimmying
Cause: *Costia, Cyclochaeta,* or *Chilodonella* parasites
Treatment: Use a commercial remedy of malachite green and do frequent water changes.

Swim Bladder Disease

Occurrence: Infrequent
Symptoms: Abnormal swimming patterns or loss of balance
Cause: Bacterial infection, physical injury to the swim bladder from fighting or during transportation from dealer, or poor water quality
Treatment: Treat with an antibiotic in a clean, shallow tank. Change the water frequently. This disease is difficult to treat successfully.

Tuberculosis

Occurrence: Rare
Symptoms: Dull-colored body, clamped fins, weight loss, ulcers, and pop eye in some cases
Cause: *Mycobacterium* is the cause. ***Caution!*** Under the right circumstances, this disease can be transferred to humans through contact with infected fish.

Watch for any signs of irregular swimming.

Treatment: No effective aquarium treatment is available. Wear plastic gloves, remove the Betta from the tank, and euthanize it immediately. To euthanize a fish painlessly, place it in a plastic cup with a small amount of tap water and set it in the freezer. Discard, cup and all, when frozen.

Velvet

Occurrence: Very common

Symptoms: A golden-velvet or gray coating on the body or fin areas; your Betta will look like it has been sprinkled with gold dust

Cause: Adult *Oodinium* parasites will attach themselves to your Betta and then fall off after about one week. These parasites will sink down into the gravel and begin to multiply. The new parasites are then released into the water and will reinfect the fish in your aquarium.

Treatment: Use commercial malachite green remedy. Add 1 tablespoon of aquarium salt for each 5 gallons of water. Velvet does not need to be treated in a quarantine tank.

Other Causes of Disease

Poisoning

To avoid inadvertently poisoning your Betta, never allow any materials made of metal to come into contact with the aquarium water. Use only equipment designed for aquarium applications.

Household cleaners, paint, and insect sprays can be deadly if they get in the aquarium. If it becomes necessary to use these products in the vicinity of the aquarium, shut down all equipment and cover the tank with a lightweight plastic drop cloth. Remove the cover and restart the tank only when you are sure the room is back to normal. Do a partial water change the next day, to be on the safe side. A large aquarium with a valuable collection of fish and plants should be temporarily relocated for painting, construction, or any similar disruptions.

Improper Diet and Overfeeding

A balanced diet that consists of a wide variety of commercially packaged flakes, small servings of algae or veggies, and live foods such as brine shrimp and blackworms, will go far to keep your Betta healthy.

Regularly overfeeding your Betta will cause poor water conditions and threaten your Betta's health. Resist the temptation to feed too much.

Frightening Your Fishes

Sudden changes in lighting (switching on the aquarium lights while the room is still dark) can cause your Betta to panic and injure itself on decorations and tank walls as it makes a mad dash for cover. Physical damage to scales and fins will open the door for bacteria to attack. To avoid this unfortunate situation, gradually increase room lighting by opening curtains and blinds and turning on lamps before you switch on the aquarium lights.

In addition, if you constantly alter tank decorations and stick your hands into the aquarium water, your Betta will become stressed and will be at a higher risk for disease. Save these major changes for once a month, at most.

A Hospital Tank

Using your quarantine tank as a hospital tank for an ailing Betta is much better than treating your fish in its display tank. The separate tank lowers the risk of the disease spreading to other fish in the same aquarium.

Moreover, treatment with antibiotics and other medications may destroy part of the aquarium's essential bacteria and reduce the efficiency of the main tank's biological filtration system. These conditions can lead to even greater health problems and outbreaks of new diseases. A hospital tank will prevent that problem.

Before and after each use, the hospital tank and all of its equipment should be thoroughly sterilized with hot water to make sure all unwanted organisms are destroyed.

Disease can quickly spread among the fish in a community tank, so it's best to isolate a sick fish and treat it in a hospital tank.

Transfer a sick Betta in a plastic bag or large cup. A fishnet can be easily contaminated with disease.

When working with diseased fish, never use the net from the hospital tank to transport fish back into the main aquarium. All nets that are involved in the transport of ill fish should be sterilized with hot water before and after use to keep disease from spreading.

Treatment Tips

When faced with a disease problem, never run down to the local merchant to purchase several different types of medications in the hopes that one of them will work. Improperly used medications can kill your Betta as quickly as if you did nothing at all.

If you have checked out your tank and have not been able to identify the disease or its cause, get assistance. Your vet or fish dealer may be able to give you the expert advice that you will need to take care of the problem.

The Old-Fashioned Salt Bath

One of the oldest remedies for treating diseases such as ich and fungus is a saltwater bath. I have used this method for more than twenty-five years and have found that it has a high rate of success.

Simply add 1 teaspoon of kosher salt for each gallon of water in your hospital tank. Keep adding 1 teaspoon of salt twice a day for the first five days. If the infected Betta is not completely well by the fifth day, continue to add 1 teaspoon of salt for another three days.

When medication is required, follow all the instructions on the package to the letter. Avoid the temptation of adding extra medication just to be on the safe side. There are good reasons why manufacturers put specific directions and dosage amounts on the bottle or carton. Don't second-guess them.

Make sure you carry through the process of administering medication for the entire suggested time of treatment. Don't stop medicating simply because your Betta begins to look healthy again. Once you move a fish to a hospital tank, leave it there for at least two weeks after symptoms have disappeared.

The Medicine Chest

You may want to keep some basic medications and other supplies on hand, just in case.

- Copper-based medication for parasite problems
- Pair of rubber gloves for handling fish and medications
- Bottle of commercial malachite green treatment
- Small box of kosher salt
- Complete pH test kit
- Complete nitrite/nitrate test kit
- Complete ammonia test kit
- Bottle of dechlorinator
- Bottle of commercial methylene blue treatment
- Cotton swabs

Preventing disease is easier than treating it. Keep your fishes' tank clean and healthy, and your fish will be healthy and beautiful.

- Bleach to disinfect equipment
- Bottle of mercurochrome (dilute 50 percent in tap water immediately before using)
- Pair of cuticle scissors
- Pair of tweezers
- Magnifying glass
- Clean towels

By keeping up with a few maintenance routines, having a watchful eye, and understanding disease prevention practices, you can easily ensure your Bettas' good health. Consider it repayment for all the joy your fish have given you.

Chapter 10

Breeding Your Bettas

Although the average hobbyist is unlikely to make a lot of money breeding Bettas, there is much wisdom and enjoyment to be gained from this fascinating aspect of the hobby. Breeding techniques vary greatly from hobbyist to hobbyist. There is really no "perfect way" to breed a Betta. Many methods have worked well over the years, but there is always room for improvement and new ideas.

Bettas breed in two different ways. Species such as the banded Betta *(Betta taeniata)* and the painted Betta *(Betta picta)* are mouthbrooders. The male picks up the fertilized eggs and carries them in his mouth until the fry hatch and are big enough to swim freely. Other Bettas, such as the Siamese Fighting Fish *(Betta splendens)* and the peaceful Betta *(Betta imbellis)* build bubblenests. The male bears most of the responsibility here, too. He constructs the nest and guards the eggs until they hatch.

Mouthbrooders

In a mouthbrooder's native habitat, swift currents prevent the Betta from successfully building bubblenests. Instead, the male carries the eggs in his mouth, where they are incubated until they hatch.

During spawning, the female and male embrace, and eggs are deposited on the male's anal fin. Shortly after, the female will scoop them up and deposit them into her mate's waiting mouth. This cycle is then repeated until all of her eggs have been expelled. A single spawning among these species can produce as many as one hundred eggs.

After spawning, the female should be removed from the breeding tank and placed in isolation so that she can recuperate.

The Bettas' eggs will remain in the male's mouth for about five days, until they hatch. After the young fry swim away from their father's mouth, they are on their own and will not receive any further parental care. At this time, the male should be removed from the tank. Now that his parental duties are at an end and after his five-day fast, he may be tempted to devour his own young.

Nest Builders

Bettas who live in more stagnant waters build nests. The eggs of these nest builders are heavier than water and will sink.

After the female has expelled all her eggs, the male catches them before they sink to the bottom and spits them into the floating raft of bubbles he has built. This amusing catching and spitting game will continue until all the eggs are expelled.

A single spawning can produce as many as 300 eggs. They hatch in about two days. The male Betta should be removed from the tank after the hatching process is complete.

The remainder of this chapter will take a closer look at reproduction strategies and techniques among the bubblenest builders. These particular species are among the most popular of all the Bettas and are easy to breed.

This male guards his bubblenest.

The Breeding Room

If you just want to add a few more Bettas to your collection, or possibly pass a few along to your friends and family, you need only a single breeding tank and a few jars in which to store the male Bettas. The jars can be placed on a shelf underneath the breeding tank.

If you want to breed large numbers of Bettas and perhaps develop new strains, you will need a lot more room in which to work. A spare bedroom, a heated garage space, or a corner of the basement can be outfitted as a fish room. Make sure you understand the commitment before you take this step. Serious fish breeding requires a considerable investment of time and money, in addition to the space.

Separate Tanks Are Best

Bettas will often attempt to breed in a crowded environment, even in a bustling community tank filled with other species, such as Guppies and Platys. However, deliberately encouraging Bettas to breed in a community tank is not a good idea. If the male Betta decides his tankmates pose a threat, he may do quite a bit of physical damage to them in defending his territory from the perceived danger. Further, eggs and newborn fry can be eaten by the Betta's tankmates before he has a chance to save them.

Betta courtship and spawning can involve a lot of chasing and dashing madly about the tank, and other fish may end up injured simply because they were in the wrong place at the wrong time. It is much better in the long run to provide your Bettas with their own breeding tank to avoid such problems.

Selecting Breeding Stock

To start, you might want to consider breeding inexpensive Bettas so you can get a solid understanding of the basics involved in setting up a breeding tank and introducing potential mating partners. That way, you won't be risking expensive fish on beginner mistakes. But don't limit yourself by purchasing only two Bettas. If space allows, buy at least three males and three females. This gives you several pairs to work with at the same time.

If you intend to keep a large number of males for breeding purposes, space will quickly become a major consideration. It is not financially practical to keep each male and female in its own 10-gallon tank. Females can usually be grouped together in one aquarium if they are all about the same size and have sufficient hiding places.

Betta courtship can involve a lot of action. It's best done with the breeding pair in a tank by themselves.

As you have learned, two male Bettas cannot be kept together without fighting, and should be separated in gallon jars with a simple hose and airstone inserted through the lid to provide gas exchange and circulation. These jars can be placed side by side on a shelf. A piece of dark construction paper or cardboard can be inserted between each jar so that the males will not be able to see each other. Individual jars will help keep the prospective males calm and relaxed until it is time for spawning. If the Bettas are allowed to see each other, they will constantly batter their bodies against the glass and become stressed while trying to defend their imaginary territories and boundaries. If you use small jars, it is vitally important to do daily water changes to keep them clean and free from ammonia buildup.

If the female has battled with disease before spawning, she may not be able to produce strong eggs that will develop normally. Even though fry can be produced from such eggs, the youngsters will often be defective or deformed. It is important that your spawning females be in optimal health and free from disease before they are used for breeding.

Setting Up a Breeding Tank

A 10-gallon aquarium is a good starting size for a breeding tank because it allows you to carefully keep track of the bubblenest, spawning rituals, and fry. All parts of the breeding tank (glass, equipment, rocks, and the like) should be carefully cleaned with warm water and completely sterilized in a salt solution to prevent any lingering bacteria or fungus from attacking the eggs and newborn fry.

Cover the Tank

A glass cover will ensure that your spawning Bettas do not jump from the tank, and will prevent dirt and dust from entering the water. A cover will also protect the nest and eggs by keeping heat loss at the surface to a minimum.

Plants

Spawning Bettas can become aggressive, so it is always wise to purchase several thick plants for your breeding tank. The plants provide privacy, can be used in the construction of a bubblenest, and will offer shelter to the female, if necessary. Hornwort (*Ceratophyllum demersum*) is a good choice.

Decorations

Providing plants and other decorations among which your female Betta can hide will give her and the male fish an opportunity to get pleasantly acquainted before spawning. If there are no hiding places in the breeding tank, the male Betta may kill his mate out of territorial instinct before any spawning can take place.

Spawning Bettas can be aggressive. This male is putting on a threat display.

Substrate

It is best to leave the bottom of the tank bare except for a few large stones that can be placed strategically in the corner for the female's protection before, during, and after courtship.

Water Conditions

For breeding purposes, the pH of the water in the spawning tank should be between 6.8 and 7. The water should also be slightly soft, with a degree of hardness between 8 and 10. This level can usually be maintained by using a mixture of 50 percent tap water and 50 percent demineralized water. For a large breeding operation, you may need a reverse osmosis unit.

A temperature of 82 degrees Fahrenheit is standard for breeding Bettas, but should be watched closely. If the temperature rises above 85 degrees, the Betta's eggs may be severely damaged from the excess heat. Higher temperatures will also cause rapid egg development, which can produce weak or deformed fry.

The water in the breeding tank should be kept a couple of inches below the rim of the tank. This gives the fry access to warm, moist air at the surface when their labyrinth organs begin to develop.

Filtration

Water turbulence can damage the bubblenest and make it quite difficult for the male to keep the eggs or fry in the nest. Power filter outlets should be adjusted to minimize surface disturbance. You may opt to use no filtration at all. In that case, do a partial water change every other day using a small siphon that won't damage the bubblenest. In tanks smaller than 10 gallons, daily water changes will be necessary.

Conditioning Breeders

Some individual Bettas breed readily; others seem to have a hard time figuring out the program. Although no method is completely foolproof, there are several tricks you can try to encourage your Bettas to spawn.

Artificial Storms and Weather

Water changes are very important not only to the health of your Betta, but also to the Betta's success in spawning. In the wild, seasonal rains signal the start of nature's breeding system. Natural waters become softer as they are diluted with fresh rainwater, and the nitrogen level begins to drop. You can duplicate this effect by frequent water changes (about 20 percent per day for breeding). Adding demineralized water will help stimulate the Bettas to enter their seasonal spawning cycle.

An increase in barometric pressure will also condition your Bettas for breeding. Many hobbyists have reported that their Bettas are more willing to breed right before or during a rain or snowstorm. You may be able to choose a good time to introduce a pair by following the local weather reports.

The rainy season can be duplicated by showering the surface of the aquarium. Use an ordinary watering can to replace water when you are doing a water change. Another method is to pour water slowly through a colander or kitchen strainer.

In the wild, water in the paddy or pond may warm during the day, then drop as a result of rainfall in the evening. Try fluctuating the temperature of the breeding tank. Drop the temperature to around 73 degrees Fahrenheit at night and then slowly raise the temperature back up to 80 degrees during the day. You can do this when you are changing water. Use replacement water that is cooler than the tank. Experiment with a bucket and a thermometer to figure out how much cool water to add to achieve the desired temperature drop.

Feeding

Another common change in the natural environment during breeding season is the sudden abundance of live foods. Insects may be transported to the hungry fish via rainwater. And like the Bettas, aquatic invertebrates time their reproduction by the monsoons. Thus, food for the Betta is abundant when the fish needs it most.

Offer your potential spawners live brine shrimp and blackworms to condition them for breeding. When feeding live or frozen foods, do not discontinue the daily use of your Betta's standard flake foods. These manufactured foods provide additional nutrients that the Betta needs for good health and successful spawning. Live foods alone may not provide a balanced diet, especially if you have only one type available.

Competition

If you have a male that is reluctant to breed, you might try introducing a second male in a jar and placing the rival male near the spawning tank. When the first Betta realizes that there may be competition for his female, he may be inspired to breed.

If you have a male who is reluctant to breed, a little competition from another male might be just the inspiration he needs.

Getting to Know You

Bettas can be conditioned to spawn by separating the male and the female with a glass partition while live food is fed to both parties. Frequent small feedings will help the pair to reach spawning condition quickly. The sight of the female may also convince the male to begin building a bubblenest.

An alternative method is to place the female Betta in a jar and allow her to float in the breeding tank. Often, a male will be become excited just because a female is present. The glass jar will protect her from aggression and harm until the nest is complete. One disadvantage of this technique is that the female may become too excited and drop her eggs before she is released.

Introducing Bettas to the Breeding Tank

It is important to introduce the female Betta to the breeding tank before bringing in the male. Give her time to get used to her new surroundings, and then place her behind a clear tank partition or in a glass jar before you introduce the

Selective Breeding

Just around the corner lies a striking new color or fin type. But to obtain the desired results, you will need to breed your Bettas selectively.

To prepare for selective breeding, choose several Bettas that display characteristics that can be intensified to produce solid strains. A strain is a related family of Bettas that display specific characteristics that can be inherited by their offspring. These beautiful characteristics may include long fins, unusual color patterns, or other traits that appeal to your idea of what a beautiful Betta should look like.

It is important to buy a female of the same strain as the male you choose in order to strengthen the line and to save valuable time that can be better used in the pursuit of a new variation.

The breeding process used to produce a pure strain of Bettas is known as inbreeding. The first step in this process is to choose a male and a female that display a number of similar characteristics that you find interesting. After the first brood is born and raised, select a healthy male and breed him back to his mother. In the next generation, take the best quality grandson and breed him back to his grandmother, and so on for successive generations. This will help to seal the characteristics you are looking for.

As new generations are born, keep an eye out for any males born with unique characteristics that might be developed into new lines. If the female from the first generation dies, select the healthiest daughter and continue the line from that point on. Inbreeding is more effective than line breeding, which involves the mating of half-brothers and sisters.

male. Some males are more aggressive than others, and it is very difficult to know an individual male's habits before he spawns for the first time. Once the male has built a nest, the female can safely be released.

Note that if you use a divider, the male may build his nest so that it actually leans against the partition. If this happens, moving the divider may seriously damage the nest. Netting the female to place her on the other side of the divider can cause her to become too stressed to spawn. Move the female by coaxing her gently into a clear plastic cup. She can then be lifted up and over the divider.

> **TIP**
>
> **Good Plants for the Spawning Tank**
>
> Hornwort (Ceratophyllum demersum), floating or anchored
>
> Water sprite (Ceratopteris thalictroides), free floating
>
> Water hyacinth (Eichhornia crassipes), free floating
>
> Water lettuce (Pistia stratiodes), free floating
>
> Crystalwort (Riccia fluitans), floating

There is always the possibility that the female may drop her eggs before the nest is completed. This sometimes occurs when the fish can see each other but cannot interact. Such is life. You must start over with another female.

With a large, heavily planted spawning tank, you may be able to introduce both partners at the same time. If the female has enough well-covered safety areas to which she can flee, the pair may be left in the spawning tank to breed several times without any serious damage being inflicted upon the female by her partner. This situation more closely matches what occurs in the wild.

Spawning Rituals

Prior to spawning, the male Betta builds a floating nest carefully constructed out of tiny air bubbles coated with mucus from his own mouth. Some individual males also use bits of plant debris to help keep the bubbles together.

Male Bettas court their females flamboyantly. He will often spread his fins, flare his gill covers, and twist his body to impress his female companion. This beautiful display of body movement and vibrant color can last for several hours at a time and is fascinating to observe.

Female Bettas do not display the elaborate color and finnage that the males do, but they will often darken and may develop barring on their body. They may also have a papilla (white egg spot) near their belly region. A female Betta will show interest in a male by wiggling her body slowly back and forth.

This male flares his gills to impress his female.

After the male and female are placed together, a rough courtship may begin. The male will use any means possible to bring the female up to the nest, including tearing her fins. When the female reaches the nest, she will signal the male that she is ready to spawn by dipping her head downward. At this time, both fish will again flash intensified coloration.

Spawning Behavior

When mating begins, the male wraps himself around the female and expels her eggs by squeezing her. The eggs will be deposited on his anal fin. When the first spawning embrace is complete, the male will fertilize the eggs and begin to gather them up as they sink and blow the eggs into the bubblenest. He will continue to do this until they hatch, should any topple out of the nest.

Several spawning embraces may occur, with small amounts of eggs being released each time. At times, no eggs will be expelled during the embrace, but the mating will usually continue until all the eggs are released successfully. Spawning can last for several hours.

After Spawning

After spawning, the female must be moved to another tank or the male will most likely kill her. She will also need time to recuperate from the spawning ritual. There is a good chance the female's fins may be torn or ragged from the rough courtship. If she has been injured, add a small amount of malachite green medication to her water to increase her chances of fighting off disease. Place the female alone in a tank with good filtration and water quality to help her recover quickly.

The female should be allowed to remain on her own for at least one week before she is placed back into a community aquarium or with other female Bettas. She will be weak and will lack the resources or energy to defend herself from other fish as she normally would. Keep a close eye on her during this recuperation period to make sure she is recovering normally and remains disease-free.

Caring for the Eggs

For the next few days, the male will diligently guard his eggs and return to the nest any that fall out. He will also add more bubbles to the nest as he sees fit. Often he will build other nests and move the eggs around to his liking.

Your Contribution

The eggs in your breeding tank can be damaged by lack of oxygen, which will slow down their normal rate of cell division. However, it is not practical to have a large amount of aeration in the breeding tank, because the strong current will destroy the Betta's nest.

A good solution to this problem is to place a single airstone at the surface that is hooked up to a gang valve. Adjust the gang valve's knob so that the oxygen flowing to it is restricted, allowing the airstone to bubble only slightly. This will provide aeration to the tank without disturbing the nest. Intense lighting can also damage the eggs, so minimize lighting in the breeding tank.

Caring for the Fry

The eggs will hatch in twenty-four to forty-eight hours, and the young will hang, tail down, from the individual bubbles in the nest. For the thirty-six hours following birth, the fry will remain there as they absorb their yolk sacs.

During this short period after birth, carefully watch for any signs of water fungus *(Saprolegnia),* which can attack any unfertilized eggs. If left unattended, this disease can quickly spread to the fry and to the adult male who is taking care of them. To avoid this problem, carefully remove any eggs that are unfertilized or dead before the fungus has a chance to develop. Dead eggs become opaque white; developing eggs remain translucent, and dark eye spots will become evident.

Feeding the Fry

Betta fry are tiny and should be fed with liquified foods. Make sure you change the water frequently to avoid fouling the tank. *Infusoria* cultures (microscopic and near-microscopic organisms, such as protozoa) can be fed through an eye-dropper. You can find instructions for culturing fry foods in many aquarium books or online. After a few weeks have passed, baby brine shrimp can be fed to the fry to help them grow larger.

As your fry grow, they will prefer a diet more like that of their parents. A well-rounded diet should include vegetable flakes, standard flakes, live brine shrimp, dried shrimp meat, and a limited amount of live blackworms. Small offerings of finely chopped boiled spinach or fresh lettuce will be appreciated as well. If your aquarium contains live plants, the growing fry will periodically

Like many fish, Bettas may eat their young. If you leave them to spawn in the community tank, none of the fry may ever survive.

nibble on them too. Young Bettas have very delicate mouths, so do not feed them any coarse foods that can tear their sensitive tissues.

Feed the fry small meals several times a day. Remove all food that has not been eaten within five minutes. Betta fry have a long gut and eat small amounts at a time. They will be hungry again an hour or two after feeding.

Moving the Fry

Shortly after they hatch, place the young Bettas in their own container. The fry can be placed in a small tank of their own, which should be equipped just like a display tank. It is dangerous to place large power filters or other mechanical types of filtration in their grow-out tank, though, because the fry's small size leaves them vulnerable to being accidentally sucked in. Protect the filter intake with a fine mesh net, and adjust the flow carefully. Or simply use an airstone and change the water frequently, dispensing with filtration.

One of the best methods to remove fry without damaging them physically is to carefully scoop them up with a plastic cup and then slowly add water from their new tank to the cup until they have become acclimated to their new conditions. Never catch fry with a net, because their delicate bodies can be severely damaged by the nylon mesh.

Separating the Sexes

After the fry have been removed to the grow-out tank, they can stay there until you can determine their gender. At about 3 months of age, the fry will begin to show their colors and finnage. Males will be more brightly colored and have longer fins than the females. At this time, the males must be separated from each other and from the females.

The females can be placed together in a single aquarium, while the males are placed individually in 1-gallon jars. Make sure the jars have adequate aeration and clean water conditions. Frequent water changes will be necessary. After the second move, the fry can remain in their respective tanks or large jars until they reach the size of adults. Then they can be moved to regular aquariums.

Appendix

Learning More About Your Betta

One of the best ways to expand your knowledge as an aquarium keeper is to read as much as you can about your aquarium hobby so that you will keep informed about current issues and new ideas. Books from your local library are one of the greatest sources of free information you can use to supplement your aquarium skills and knowledge.

Books

Bailey, M. and G. Sandford, *The Ultimate Aquarium*, Smithmark Publishers, 1995.

Burgess P., M. Bailey, and A. Exell, *A-Z of Tropical Fish Diseases and Health Problems*, Howell Book House, 1999.

Gratzek, J.B., *Aquariology: Fish Diseases and Water Chemistry*, Tetra Press, 1992.

Hargrove, Maddy and Mic Hargrove, *Aquariums For Dummies*, John Wiley & Sons, 1999.

Hiscock, P., *Creating a Natural Aquarium*, Howell Book House, 2000.

James, B.A., *Fishkeeper's Guide to Aquarium Plants*, Salamander Books, 1986.

Ostrow, Michael, *Bettas*, TFH Publications, 1989.

Scheurmann, Ines, *The Natural Aquarium Handbook*, Barron's, 1990.

Skomal, Gregory, *Freshwater Aquarium: Your Happy Healthy Pet*, Howell Book House, 2005.

Magazines

Product information changes quickly, as constantly advancing technology is put to use in the design of more efficient aquarium systems and equipment. New products appear on the market every month. To keep up with rapidly changing aquarium technology, beginning hobbyists can rely on magazines to supply new information. These magazines will give you an even firmer foundation in aquarium basics and will help you start on new adventures of aquatic exploration. You will also find many articles and tidbits of information concerning Bettas and their care in all of these publications.

Aquarium Fish Magazine
P.O. Box 6050
Mission Viejo, CA 92690-6050
(949) 855-8822
www.aquariumfish.com

FAMA: Freshwater and Marine Aquarium
P.O. Box 6050
Mission Viejo, CA 92690-6050
(949) 855-8822
www.famamagazine.com

Practical Fishkeeping
Bretton Court
Bretton
Peterborough
Cambridgeshire
PE3 8DZ
www.practicalfishkeeping.co.uk

Tropical Fish Hobbyist
One TFH Plaza
Neptune City, NJ 07753
(800) 631-2188
www.tfhmagazine.com

Internet Resources

Typing the words "Betta aquarium fish" into a search engine recently resulted in 736,000 hits. Clearly, a wealth of information on Bettas can be found on the Internet. Narrowing my search to *"Betta splendens"* gave me about 220,000 hits. All the sites listed here offer links to dozens more.

Aqua Link
www.aqualink.com
This site includes articles and forums about maintaining an aquarium, and a huge store for aquarium supplies.

Aquaria Central
www.aquariacentral.com
Chat rooms, forums, articles, and supplies for the aquarium hobbyist.

Bettatalk
www.Bettatalk.com
This is the largest Betta site on the Web, and includes everything from buying and raising Bettas to Betta art and news.

FishBase
www.fishbase.org
An essential Web site for all fishkeepers, FishBase offers loads of information on more than 29,000 species.

Fish Index
www.fishindex.com
A neat feature of this general information site is the conversion tools that help you figure the volume of odd-shaped tanks, metric equivalents, and more.

Fish Link Central
www.fishlinkcentral.com
A super-link page that will bring you to all kinds of aquarium resources on the Internet.

Majestic Bettas
www.majesticBettas.com
This informative Web site for Betta breeders and hobbyists includes the history of *Betta splendens,* advice on care, and sources for supplies.

Clubs and Organizations

Clubs and organizations offer many opportunities to learn more about proper Betta care. The International Betta Congress (IBC) is dedicated to developing new strains of Bettas and sharing information on improving Betta care.

The IBC publishes articles on all aspects of Betta care, including proper nutrition, disease prevention and treatment, and breeding. The IBC also provides helpful information on Betta shows, mailing lists, and pictures of new strains.

The International Betta Congress
255 Station Road
Quakertown, PA 18951
(215) 536-1906
www.ibcBettas.org

Index

acidity, pH value checking, 62–63
acrylic tanks, purchasing, 43
adding fish to tank, timeline, 65
aeration, systems, 60–61
aggression, fighting fish, 13–15
air pumps, 60
airstones, 61
algae, 90–91
alkalinity, pH, 62–63
Amazon swords (*Echinodorus* species),
     69–70
ammonia, nitrogen cycle, 63–64
anacharis (*Elodea densa*), 69
anal fin, 10, 20–21
anatomy, 10, 12, 17–26
appetite loss, reasons for, 91
aquariums
     accessory equipment, 53–55
     acrylic tanks, 43
     aeration systems, 60–61
     breeding tanks, 109, 110–112
     capacity, 44–46
     covers, 53–54, 111
     decorations, 58–60
     dividers, 42
     egglayers, 36
     emptying before moving, 57
     environmental guidelines, 15–16
     filtration systems, 47–51
     financial considerations, 40–41
     fish addition timeline, 65
     fish-per-tank calculations, 79–80
     glass tanks, 43
     heaters, 51–52
     home built cautions/concerns, 43

lifestyle preferences, 19
lifting guidelines, 59
lighting, 52–54
livebearers, 36
location considerations, 42
maintenance, 94–95
new fish introduction techniques, 83
new tank syndrome, 82
nitrogen cycle, 63–64
overstocking, 78, 80–81
plants, 66–75
prefill cleaning, 57
quarantine tanks, 83, 103–104
secondhand considerations, 45
shape/type, 43–44
size, 41, 44–45
stands, 56–58
substrates, 46–47
tankmate suggestions, 14–15, 34–37
thermometers, 52
water conditioning, 61–63
water temperature preferences, 12
aquascaping, 68
arrowhead (*Sagittaria* species), 70
artificial tank storms, 112–113

baby Guppies, food source, 87
bacterial septicemia, 96
Banded Betta (*Betta taeniata*), 33
Barbs, tankmate, 14–15
baths, saltwater, 105
behaviors, health indicators, 93
bicolored Betta, 33
biological filtration, 48

Blue Gourami *(Trichogaster trichopterisi)*, 37
body shapes, 17–18
bottom-feeders, terminal mouth, 18
breeding, 107–113, 115–120
  competition, 113
  rituals, 116–118
  tanks, 109–110–112
  weather, 112–113
Brunei Betta *(Betta macrostoma)*, 29–30
bubblenests, 108
butterfly Betta, 33

Cambodian Betta, 33
Cambodian-butterfly Betta, 33–34
canister filters, 49
capacity, aquarium, 44–46
carbohydrates, 87
Catfish, 18, 35–36
caudal fin, 10, 20–21
chemical filtration, 48
chlorine, 62
Cichlids, tankmate concerns, 15
Climbing Perch *(Anabas testudineus)*, 12
Clown Rasboras *(Rasbora kalochroma)*, 37
colors, 21, 33–34
constipation, 96
Coolie Loach *(Pangio kuhlii)*, tankmate, 35
corner box filters, 47–48
covers, aquarium, 53–54, 111
Croaking Gourami *(Trichopsis,* species), 37
crypts *(Cryptocoryne* species), 70
currents, quiet preferences, 12

Danios, tankmate, 14
dealers, 76–79
decorations, 58–60, 111
dH values, water conditioning, 63
diet, improper, 103. *See also* foods
disease, reference guide, 100. *See also* health problems
dividers, aquarium, 42

dorsal fin, 10, 20–21
dropsy, 97
Dwarf Croaking Gourami *(Trichopsis pumila)*, 37
Dwarf Gourami *(Colisa lalia)*, 37

ears, 24
earthworms, food source, 90
Edith's Betta *(Betta edithae)*, 29
eelgrasses *(Vallisneria* species), 70–71
egglayers, 36
electrical outlets, stand/tank location, 57
Emerald Betta *(Betta smaragdina)*, 30–31
eyes, 10, 23–24

feeding schedules, 87
females, 14, 107–118, 120
fertilizers, plant foods, 75
fighting fish, territorial, 13–15
filtration systems, 47–51, 112
  canister filters, 49
  corner box filters, 47–48
  fluidized bed filters, 50–51
  power filters, 48–49
  sponge filters, 51
  undergravel filters, 50
fin rot, 97
fins, 10, 20–21, 24–25
  anal fin, 10, 20–21
  caudal (tail) fin, 10, 20–21
  dorsal fin, 10, 20–21
  pectoral fins, 10, 20–21
  ventral (pelvic) fins, 10, 20–21
fish lice, 97–98
flakes, food type, 88
flooring, stand/tank location, 56–58
fluidized bed filters, 50–51
fluorescent bulbs, 52–53
Foershi's Betta *(Betta foershi)*, 29
foods, 75, 86–91, 103, 113, 119–120
freeze-dried foods, 90
fright, 103
frozen foods, 89
frozen seafood, food source, 87

fry, care guidelines, 118–120
fungus, 98

gill parasites, 99
Glass Catfish (Kryptopterus bicirrhus), 35
glass tanks, 43
Goodeidae livebearers, 36
Gouramis (Trichogaster, Colisa), 12, 37
gravel (substrate), 46–47, 58, 68, 112
Guppies, 18, 36, 87

hardness, water, 63
Harlequin Rasbora (Rasbora heteromorpha), 36
health, 77–79, 91–93, 105–106
health problems, 96–105. See also specific
problems
hearing, 10, 24
heaters, 51–52
Hemirhamphidae, livebearers, 36
hornwort (Ceratopyllum demersum),
70–71
hygro (Hygrophila species), 71–72

ich, 99
incandescent lighting, 52
insects, food source, 87
intestinal parasites, 99

Java fern (Microsorium species), 71, 73

labyrinth fish (Anabantidae), 12
labyrinth organ, 12, 25–26
lateral line, 10, 24
Libby Betta, 13
light hoods, 53–54
lighting, 52–54, 75, 83
    fluorescent bulbs, 52–53
    incandescent, 52
    metal halide bulbs, 53
livebearers, 36
live foods, 90
Loaches, 36

maintenance, 94–95
males, 13–15, 42, 107–110, 113–118,
120
marbled Betta, 34
mechanical filtration, 48
medical supplies, 105–106
metal halide bulbs, 53
Microsorium species (Java fern), 71, 73
minerals, 86–87
Mollies, 36
mosquito larvae, food source, 89
mouthbrooders, 107–108
Mouthbrooding Betta (Betta pugnax),
30–31
mouth fungus, 99–100
mouth structure, 18, 24–25

nest builders, 108
nests, territorial aggression, 13–15
nets, 54
new tank syndrome, 82
nitrates, 64
nitrites, water monitoring, 63–64
nitrogen cycle, 63–64
non-submersible heaters, 51–52
nostrils, 10, 24–25
nutrition requirements, 86–87
Nymphaea species (water lilies), 73–74

orientation, light interpretation, 23
osmosis, 23
overfeeding, 103
overstocking, aquarium, 78, 80–81
ownership, popularity, 11

Painted Betta (Betta picta), 29
Pangio kuhlii (Coolie Loach), 35
Paradise Fishes (Macropodus), 12
Peaceful Betta (Betta imbellis), 29
Pearl Gourami (Trichogaster leeri), 37
Pearly Betta (Betta anabatoides), 28
pectoral fins, 10, 20–21
pellets, food type, 89
pelvic (ventral) fins, 10, 20–21

pH values, 62–63
plants, 66–75, 90–91, 111, 116. *See also*
    specific species
Platys, 18, 36
Poeciliidae, livebearers, 36
poisoning, 102–103
pop eye, 100
power filters, 48–49
protein, 87
pumps, air, 60
Pygmy Rasbora *(Rasbora matculatus),* 37

quarantine tanks, 83, 103–104

Rasboras *(Rasbora spp.),* 14, 35–37
Red-Tailed Rasbora *(Rasbora borapetensis),*
    36
respiratory system, 12, 22, 25–26
rocks, aquarium decorations, 58–59

Sagittaria species (arrowhead), 70
saltwater baths, 105
Sarawak Betta *(Betta akarensis),* 28
scales, 19
Scissortail Rasbora *(Rasbora trilineata),* 36
scrapers, 54
seafood (frozen), food source, 87
sensory organs, 23–25
shipping bags, transportation, 81–83
Siamese Fighting Fish *(Betta splendens),*
    13–14, 17, 30–33
siphons, 55
skeletal system, 22–23
sleep periods, frequency, 24
Slender Betta *(Betta bellica),* 28
slime coat, 101
slime disease, 101
smell, 10, 24–25
solid-colored Betta, 33
spawning, 107–108, 116–120
sponge filters, 51
sponges, aquarium accessory, 53
stands, 56–58
stress, 96

styrofoam, tank support, 57
submersible heaters, 51–52
substrate. *See* gravel
superior mouth, surface-feeders, 18
surface-feeders, superior mouth, 18
swim bladder, 19–20, 101
Swordtails, 36

tail (caudal) fin, 10, 20–21
tank capacity, 79–80
tankmates, 14–15, 34–37
tanks. *See* aquariums
taste, 10, 24–25
temperatures, 12, 51–52, 62, 64, 75
terminal mouth, bottom-feeders, 18
territorial fish, fighting trait, 13–15
Tessy's Betta *(Betta tussyae),* 32–33
test kits, 55
Thailand, homeland waters, 12
thermometers, 52
transporting fish, 81–92, 120
tuberculosis, 101–102
tubing, aeration system, 61

undergravel filters, 50

Vallisneria species (eelgrasses), 70–71
velvet, 102
ventral (pelvic) fins, 10, 20–21
vision, 10, 23–24
vitamins, 86

water, 61–63, 75
water conditioning, breeding tanks, 112
water currents, 12
water hardness, 63
water lettuce *(Pistia stratiodes),* 73
water lilies *(Nymphaea* species), 73–74
water sprite *(Ceratopteris* species), 74
water temperatures, 12, 51–52, 62
weather, breeding, 112–113
wood, aquarium decoration, 59–60
worms, food source, 87